Empower Your Business to Reach Its Full Potential

Empower Your Business To Reach Its Full Potential

YOUR ROAD MAP TO PLANNING AND EXECUTING A SUCCESSFUL BUSINESS

First Edition

Frank Haarlander

F. Bryan Haarlander

ISBN: 1507525117
ISBN 13: 9781507525111

DEDICATION

We dedicate this book to Frank E. Haarlander, our beloved father and grandfather, who passed away on January 1, 2015 before this book was published. The sacrifices that he made for us and the values he lived by helped us achieve our dreams. He will always hold a special place in our hearts.

DISCLAIMERS

This book is designed to provide educational information regarding the subject matters covered. While all attempts have been made to verify information provided in this book, the authors do not assume any responsibility for errors, inaccuracies, or omissions. Any perceived slights of people or organizations are unintentional.

This book is written with the understanding that the authors are not engaged in rendering legal, tax, accounting, financial, investment or any other advice related to your individual situation by publishing this book. Laws change rapidly, and you want to make sure when you implement a plan that it is based on the most current information available. You also need to be aware of the various laws governing business transactions or other business practices in your particular state or locality.

Before implementing any of the topics discussed in this book or any book, you should always first consult with a competent advisor to discuss your personal financial or business situation.

ABOUT THE AUTHORS

Frank Haarlander is a CPA (certified public accountant) who has over forty years of experience working with business and individual clients. He earned his undergraduate degree in business administration from Rutgers College in New Brunswick, NJ. After graduating from college, Frank taught sixth graders at a public elementary school for two years. He then earned his MBA at the Rutgers Professional School of Accounting in Newark, NJ, one of the country's best. Graduates from this school have traditionally gone on to public accounting jobs with one of the "Big-Eight" public accounting firms (now the "Big-Four" due to mergers). Frank was no exception. He started his business career with Lybrand, Ross Brothers & Montgomery in Philadelphia. The firm changed its name shortly afterwards to Coopers & Lybrand (C&L). Today, that firm is known as PricewaterhouseCoopers, LLP. In those days, all non-attorneys were required to start their career on the audit (attest) staff. Frank was assigned as a member of the team that would audit publicly held companies and issue an opinion on their financial statements.

While in graduate school, Frank was most interested in the courses that dealt with taxes. The instructor would discuss the fact pattern of a case, the law, the IRS regulations, and other announcements and ask the class to opine on the decision. It was a true learning experience! Frank was truly amazed that so much gray material existed between the black and white of the tax law. He realized that rather than accepting the status quo, a creative tax person may be able to make a significant impact on their client's tax liabilities. Accordingly after working a couple of years as a C&L auditor, Frank requested a transfer to the tax department of C&L. For the next four years he learned the U.S. tax system, then after six years with C&L, Frank began his career in the corporate world.

For the following 22 years, he held the position of Director of Taxes or Vice President of Taxes for some of this country's largest companies. The last corporate position he held was directing the tax department of one of GE Capital's subsidiaries.

During his years working for these companies, he earned a Masters in Tax degree from the Schools of Law and Commerce at Villanova University; as well as a designation of Green Belt instructor in the Six Sigma training method. For those who are unfamiliar with "6σ," the appellation refers to the management approach that grew out of Japan's manufacturing companies in the 1980s. The Six Sigma approach involves methodical use of analytical and statistical tools to produce quality products, improve efficiency, and limit failure rates at large organizations.

Along with his son Bryan, Frank founded a tax and accounting practice in 2001. During this time, Frank earned certifications as a Certified Asset Protection Planner™ and Certified Wealth Preservation Planner™. His education continues today by reading every available book on financial planning, wealth building, asset protection, and marketing. Frank is a member of the Pennsylvania Institute of CPAs (PICPA), American Society of Tax Problem Solvers (ASTPS), and the National Society of Accountants (NSA).

Frank is a former member of the American Institute of CPAs (AICPA), Wealth Preservation Institute, and the Asset Protection Society, where he was a Pennsylvania state representative for the group. He has held various executive positions and has served on the Board of Directors of the Philadelphia Chapter of the Tax Executives Institute. He has also served as an adjunct instructor at undergraduate accounting and graduate tax programs at local Philadelphia colleges and universities; and he speaks before the Chamber of Commerce and other business associations on various tax and business topics.

Frank is a member of SCORE, a nonprofit association of the Small Business Association (SBA) that is dedicated to helping business owners through education and training to get started, grow, and achieve their goals. As a member of SCORE, Frank mentors business owners on tax and financial matters and makes presentations to business owners on various topics.

Frank has also served in the community as a member of Paoli Hospitals' Planned Giving Committee.

F. Bryan Haarlander is a co-founder of Keystone Financial Solutions, P.C. He has been providing tax and accounting services to business owners and individuals since 2001. Bryan is an Enrolled Agent who is licensed by the Internal Revenue Service to represent taxpayers before the IRS.

Bryan earned his bachelor's degree in Hotel and Restaurant Management from Penn State University. He began his business career in the hospitality industry. He has held various positions in the restaurant industry, ranging from working with family-owned businesses to managing the operations of national chains. Because of his vast experience and expertise in the hospitality industry, he works closely with restaurant and bar owner clients.

Before co-founding our CPA firm, Bryan started and managed an office for one of the major national tax preparation companies. Bryan's office later became one of the top-producing franchisees. During those years, he served as an instructor for tax preparers to teach them how to prepare personal income tax returns and was awarded certificates of accomplishment for his extensive knowledge of the Internal Revenue Code. Bryan is a member of the American Society of Tax Problem Solvers (ASTPS).

Bryan is also the founder and president of Keystone Wealth Strategies, LLC, a financial planning advisory firm that focuses on asset protection, wealth preservation, college planning, retirement planning, and increasing the net worth of individuals. He is licensed in Pennsylvania and New Jersey to sell annuity and insurance products, has earned his Series 65 certification, and is a former member of the National Institute of Certified College Planners.

Bryan's wealth management experience has been of immense value to clients of Keystone Financial Solutions, P.C.

ACKNOWLEDGEMENTS

I want to take this opportunity to thank the many people who have encouraged me to write this book and who have provided me with the support and values that enabled me to do so.

First and foremost, I want to thank Sharon, my lovely wife and my best friend. We have been married over 40 years. She's been my motivation and sounding board for writing this book. Whenever she's listened to me as I've criticized the popular advice of pundits, seminar leaders, or TV and radio financial advisors, each time she backed me up, saying, "You should write a book." Eventually, she said it so many times that I began to believe her.

But writing a book isn't easy. The process meant spending long hours in the office away from her, which neither of us found appealing. I truly appreciate the sacrifices she has made to allow me to write this book, and I am so grateful for her continued words of encouragement.

I also am very fortunate to have my son, Frank Bryan Haarlander, to work with me for the past 13 years. His contributions to the writing of this book cannot be overstated. He helped write several of the chapters, edited others for content, details, and accuracy, and made numerous valuable suggestions. Bryan has a very different perspective than mine in his views about life and financial matters. This process has been a case of the father learning from the son (and hopefully the son learning from the father). Bryan and his wife Tara began planning for my grandson Jake's future almost immediately upon learning that she was pregnant. There were the analyses of purchasing a home, life and disability insurance needs, and planning for the funding of Jake's college education. When Sharon and I had our two children, I do not recall us paying the same degree of attention to these financial matters. I commend Bryan and Tara for taking charge of their financial responsibilities so early in life. I also want to thank them ever so much for bringing Jake into this world. I love spending every minute with him and seeing how hungry he is to learn.

Frank wishes to thank his father and mother, Frank and Wanda Haarlander, happily married for 68 years, for their love and support. After serving in the U.S. Navy in World War II, my father opted not to use his GI benefit package to attend college. Realizing that he missed an opportunity to be the first in his family to attend college, my parents saw to it that I was the first Haarlander to earn a college degree. My father has always believed that the best education is from the "College of Hard Knocks." He always believed that, while we will all make mistakes during our lifetime, we should not be discouraged. It takes a truly intelligent person to learn from his mistakes. Alumni of the "College of Hard Knocks" may continue to make mistakes, but these will be related to new ventures. The only way you don't graduate from this illustrious college is by continuing to make the same mistakes. With this book, we hope to help our readers spend less time learning from their mistakes and more time doing the things that count.

I wish to thank Bob Fedor, Gerry Francis, and George Edwards of the West Chester, Pennsylvania chapter of SCORE of the U.S. Small Business Association for allowing me to mentor business owners and make tax and accounting presentations to these owners. Ted Nichols of SCORE assisted me to better understand the loan application process as seen through the eyes of a former bank lending-officer. I appreciate the opportunity to co-mentor with Charlie Espenlaub, Jim Friedman, and John Nelson of SCORE, who know so much about the needs of small-business owners, who provide valuable advice to their clients, and whose contributions to this book were invaluable.

Finally, we'd like to acknowledge the editing help we received from Brendon Butler at *Edited Better*. Brendon's tweaks and suggestions made a great difference in helping us polish and revise the manuscript. We'd recommend his work to anybody seeking help with contract editing: editedbetter@gmail.com.

INTRODUCTION

We have worked with hundreds of business owners and individual clients in our certified public accounting (CPA) firm, Keystone Financial Solutions, P.C. Thus, we have years of first-hand experience working with business owners and the issues they face.

We have had the opportunity to work with a few from the very start of their business ventures, helping them understand the metrics of their businesses and how to better manage their profits and cash flows. We have received much satisfaction in working with these owners to help them successfully grow their businesses.

Many of our existing clients came to us after finding that their former accountants were unresponsive to their needs; after realizing that the accountant seemed unsure with their own tax advice; or discovering the hard way that the tax advice given was not correct. It always amazes us to see such incorrect advice that is offered by some in the tax profession. This point is discussed further in Chapter 5 when we share our thoughts on how to choose your team of trusted advisors.

During the course of our work with large numbers of new and existing businesses, we have identified common characteristics among businesses that were ultimately not successful. These characteristics are discussed in Chapter 3. Most of the "how-to" books on starting a business focus on a few common reasons why businesses fail. But when writing this book, we've deviated from the majority—instead of writing about a few general reasons for a failed business, we have drawn from our 14 years of experience working with all types of businesses, and we've included *specific* anecdotal examples so you can learn from the mistakes of others. We want to empower our readers to challenge conventional thinking, and we want to help you realize that there are alternative ways to start your own business.

It was through my volunteer work with SCORE that I met some of these entrepreneurs. For those who may not be familiar with SCORE, it is an acronym for Service Corps of Retired Executives, which is part of the U.S. Small Business Administration. SCORE has active and retired business leaders who volunteer their time to help and advise business owners. With such a great resource available to a business owner, it is surprising that more owners do not take advantage of this **free** and valuable resource. In addition to these free mentoring sessions for the entrepreneur who wishes to start up a new business, these mentoring services are available to existing business owners who want to grow their business, expand overseas, or address a specific problem with running their business. SCORE also provides educational programs and presentations on various topics to educate the business community and to better enable business owners to succeed.

As SCORE has grown in size to meet the needs of the business owner, its mentors have expanded beyond retired executives to include current business owners and experienced practicing consultants such as myself. Through SCORE, I have had the pleasure of co-counseling with several excellent mentors with diverse backgrounds.

Unfortunately during my mentoring sessions with SCORE and in our CPA practice, we have seen business owners plunge into starting a business without any due diligence, research, advice or mentoring from others who have already trod the same path. Examples include:

- A business owner who signed a 5-year lease with a personal guarantee because the owner did not want to lose a perfect retail store location for the business. Unfortunately, the business owner had yet to analyze whether his business plan was viable, or if he could procure the funds needed to operate the business.
- A potential entrepreneur whose business plan showed that his start-up business would generate $2 million of revenues

per month, beginning in the very first month when the business opened, and continuing without any deviation for the following 23 months.

- Start-up business with hundreds of SKUs (stock keeping units/separate inventory items) that would need to be stocked in inventory to open for business, necessitating an enormous amount of capital to purchase the inventory and a warehouse to stock those goods. The owner did not have a warehouse nor did he have the financial resources to procure or to maintain the inventory.
- A business that was started because the owner enjoyed doing something as a hobby and wanted to turn it into a company even though there was not sufficient consumer need (or even potential demand) for the product.
- The owner whose first step to start a business was to obtain an EIN from the IRS because he had read somewhere that this was an important step and in doing so failed to recognize that he was electing how he would be taxed for IRS purposes.
- A business person who used $80,000 of a home equity loan to start a business—and then could not identify how that money was spent—resulting in $80,000 of lost tax deductions because he could not document how he spent the money.

Fortunately (and, unfortunately) it is easy to start your own business. Excited to become their own boss, many potential business owners just plunge in, like they were jumping into a swimming pool for the first time. Of course, this method results in either you sinking, or you'll struggle and swallow some water and eventually make it to the side of the pool. But why take the risk of drowning, essentially throwing your money and your time down the drain because of a hasty plunge? Most people would likely agree that it would make sense to first take swimming lessons before jumping into the pool. Likewise, it is important that the entrepreneur-spirited person first take prudent precautionary steps before taking the plunge into starting a business.

Starting a new business the correct way is not easy. It requires an open mind and a willingness to make a commitment of your time and financial resources. Since we believe that it is important to follow an orderly process when starting your business, we did our best to arrange the chapters in this book in the progressive steps we believe should be followed to best fit the needs of most entrepreneurs. These steps are by no means sacrosanct or set in stone. We realize that the reader may find it advantageous to alter the order to fit particular needs or timelines.

When writing this book, the co-authors were challenged by the use of the words "I" and "we." Accordingly, to avoid any confusion by our readers, all first person references in this book pertain to Frank Haarlander. Otherwise, the authors are referring to themselves, Frank and Bryan Haarlander.

We have referred to business owners, professional advisors and others in the masculine tense. This was done purely as a matter of convenience when writing. We realize that many successful business owners and professionals are women, so we ask our female readers not to take offense. If there is any solace, keep in mind that some of the stories we have shared were the actual failures of male business owners.

Too many businesses fail because of the initial start-up and (lack of) planning. Keep in mind that all buildings are only as strong as their foundations. If you have a strong foundation, in other words, if you take the proper steps in starting your business, you will substantially increase the odds of success. While everyone would likely agree that one doesn't erect a building without first purchasing the land and making sure you have a clear title to the property and it is properly zoned, it is surprising how many businesses get started without the hard questions being asked. The hard questions that need to be asked before creating a legal entity include:

- Am I starting a business or a hobby?
- What is needed to make the business successful?
- What are the risks?
- What is my business plan telling me?

We decided to write this book to better enable small-business owners reach their maximum potentials for financial success, to build wealth, and to preserve that wealth. We want the business owner to understand that you can run the business, or you can let the business run your life. While many a business owner will state that he does not have the time to address certain aspects of his business, the successful business owners have realized that they **must make the time**.

We have arranged this book into four parts. We believe these four parts relate to the life cycle of a business, which begins with the start of the business, growing the business, measuring the financial success of the business, and then exiting from the business. These are four key steps to a financially successful business.

Part One focuses on how to start your own business. We not only discuss the action steps to start your own business, but also if you possess the characteristics of an entrepreneur (Chapter 3), how to ascertain if you have a viable business concept (Chapter 6), whether you should start your own business or buy an existing business, whether you are a good candidate for a franchise (Chapter 7), how to write the very important business plan (Chapter 8), how to finance your business (Chapter 9), and the different types of legal and tax entities (Chapters 10 & 11).

Part Two explores the financial health and tax compliance of the business. It will better enable you to determine if your business is healthy and steps you can take to improve the financial health of your business. In Chapters 12 to 16, we will address many of the record-keeping requirements that you must abide by to ensure compliance with the IRS's tax rules and regulations and how to avoid IRS collection efforts against business owners who fail to comply.

Part Three addresses how to grow your business. This section of the book (Chapters 17 & 18) should be of interest to both start-up and existing business owners. The business owner needs to continuously evaluate how the business is doing and adjust to changing market conditions and consumer needs and demands. Is the capital (money) invested in the business providing a good rate of return? Do you understand the metrics or drivers of the business that impact your cash flows and profit margins? Are you operating with a budget, and have you set realistic goals for your business?

Part Four is the final step of the business and is found in Chapter 19. It is often called the "Exit Strategy." What are your plans as to how to exit the business that you have built? Will you be leaving it to your children? Will you be selling it? How do you ascertain the value of your business? What happens to the business if you die prematurely? When someone starts a new business, almost all of his attention is focused on just that— how to start the business. It is also important that an exit strategy be considered for reasons explained in Part Four.

We have also included an Appendix section that will include items of significant interest to some, but perhaps not to all of our readers.

To get the most benefit from this book, we recommend that you first scan through the book looking at the chapter titles and the sub-headings within the chapters. This should give you a good idea as to the progressive steps and the information provided within. Next, we recommend that you read the entire book. Once you have finished reading, it would be a good idea to go back through and highlight those paragraphs that you wish to refer to again. We then suggest you focus on the chapter that represents the stage at which your business has progressed, which is hopefully Chapter One.

TABLE OF CONTENTS

Part One
Starting You
Own Business

CHAPTER 1

How You Can Profit By Reading This Book

If you are going on vacation by car, you will likely use a map or a GPS (global positioning system) system to guide you to your destination. If you are building a home, the architect or builder will use a blueprint. If you are starting your own business or if you have an existing business that you wish to "reinvent," you need a similar tool to guide you towards financial success. We hope that by reading this book you will find such guidance.

If you are starting your own business, this book is written to address some of the more significant planning considerations you will need to address. Unfortunately, many new business owners are unaware of many of the most important aspects of starting a business. Thus, they will find starting and growing their business and achieving financial success to be much more difficult than those who follow a well-thought out plan. Although some owners spend numerous hours working each week, they may find their start-up business is always a struggle. Eventually, these owners realize that their businesses are actually running their lives rather than vice versa.

Existing business owners can also benefit from reading this book. Some owners become too comfortable with the status quo. They have always done things a certain way and they find change difficult or do not realize there are more efficient or tax effective ways to run a business. When we have had the opportunity to meet with these owners and ask them if they would be interested in hearing ideas for generating improved profit margins, developing cash flows, or reducing taxes, they often respond that they already have a tax consultant or business advisor and therefore would not be interested in meeting. We've never understood this mindset. If an experienced business advisor is willing to meet with you to share some ideas with you, particularly if it is a free, no-obligation consultation, why not make the time? What do you have to lose aside from 30 minutes?

On the other hand, we as business advisors realize that we do not know everything. We are very proud of the value that our expertise can bring to clients, but we are always receptive to listening to the ideas and strategies proposed by other advisors. A very good day for us is when we learn something new and can share it with our clients. We believe existing business owners owe it to themselves and their families to listen to new ideas and to explore their merits.

Our experience has been that business owners can achieve greater financial success if they develop a strong team of trusted advisors who can mentor the owner when making key decisions and to better understand the business metrics that drive the business. Do you have a great team of advisors whom you are not using? Have the challenges of your business outgrown your current advisors? Do you understand the metrics of your business, the drivers of your cash flows and profits? It's often said that the definition of insanity is to do the same thing over and over again while expecting different results. If you expect different results, you will need to make changes. You can start by re-evaluating what you are currently doing. Do you thoroughly understand the trends of your industry? If so, do you understand how best to adjust your business to these changes? What does your target or ideal customer expect today? Do you understand what your competition is doing? What are the financials of your business trying to tell you? Have you recently met with your team of advisors to obtain their input about your current situation and best plan to proceed?

My wife was a very devoted elementary school teacher. Sharon worked extremely hard every day to educate her second grade students. Like most school teachers, she was grossly underpaid for the number of hours she worked, as well as for the responsibility she carried for educating her students. She was very good at what she did. Sharon spent a significant amount of time teaching her second-graders to consider every point of view in an open-minded way, to be responsible for their actions, and to think for themselves rather than simply follow the crowd without thinking. Unfortunately, somewhere along the way from elementary school to adulthood, the thirst for knowledge among many students, now entrepreneurs and business owners, has waned. When does the youthful thirst for knowledge and learning deteriorate to the dogmatic views that often take over our decision-making when we grow up?

You can benefit from reading this book if you can try to remain open-minded and think for yourself rather than follow the crowd. We've all heard that knowledge is power, and it's true, but to gain that knowledge you have to be open to learning new things. We suggest that you might very well benefit from the advice in this book. Of course we don't have all the answers, and we make no such claims. In our own lives, we continue to learn every day. In the same way, it's likely that you or your current advisors do not have all the answers. Thus, the responsibility is yours to learn as much as possible about ways to run your business and to increase its value. We hope that this book is the motivating seed to rekindle that thirst for knowledge within you and help you transform yourself and your business into wealth and success.

CHAPTER 2

Why Are You Starting Your Own Business?

L et's start with the premise that you have decided to start your own business. There are a multitude of reasons why a person becomes a small-business owner. Which profile fits you?

It may have been your lifetime dream to own a coffee shop or antique shop and you have decided that now is the time. You have already saved a nice retirement nest egg, and rather than continue to work in a job you are not particularly in love with, you decide to pursue your dream vocation.

You have a hobby (baking) or a passion (bicycling) and have decided to turn your hobby or passion into a business by opening a bakery or bicycle shop.

You may be already employed by a small-business owner, and you know that you could do a much better job of running this type of business. You may feel that your employer is not very intelligent, disrespects his employees, treats the customers with indifference, mismanages the business; or simply that you're undervalued and underpaid. Whatever the motivating factor, you feel that you have the requisite skills and knowledge to do a much better job than he does.

You may have lost your corporate job due to downsizing, or perhaps for a host of reasons you voluntarily left the "corporate world." The idea to start your own business may slowly be gathering momentum because, for whatever the reason, whether it's the economy, your age, education, or overseas outsourcing, you cannot find employment. The reason you lost your job is not the key issue. The driving force is that you cannot find gainful employment and you need to pay the mortgage and buy groceries. Thus, you have decided to market your skills as a contractor or consultant to the industry that you know so much about.

You are approached by a family member who wants you to join in his business venture, or who asks you to invest in an idea. Since this is family, you implicitly trust or feel compelled to assist the person for reasons of familial honor or fidelity.

Whatever the reason, when you consider starting your own business, you're sure to discuss the idea with family and friends. Friends and family will typically encourage you, the budding entrepreneur, to pursue your business venture. They all tell you that you will undoubtedly be successful. While such words of encouragement are motivational and certainly appreciated, it is also important that you speak with experts who have the experience to provide you with a *realistic* evaluation of your idea. Only an impartial judge can be trusted to provide you with an impartial response regarding the potential success of your idea.

While there are numerous motivations behind your choice to start your own business, the fact is that you are committed. You *are* going to move forward with your plan. Let's begin with that premise.

CHAPTER 3

Do You Have the Necessary Characteristics to Succeed?

Many persons are familiar with the Myers-Briggs type indicator (MBTI) assessment test. It is a psychometric questionnaire designed to measure psychological preferences in how people perceive the world and make decisions. These preferences are based on the theories proposed by Carl Gustav Jung. Jung theorized that there are four principal psychological functions by which our personalities experience the world. He found that people tend to develop a certain style of communication and social interaction that reflects their personality. They are more likely to connect with those who have similar traits; likewise, people have a more difficult time connecting with those whose personalities are different. Jung wrote that everyone has elements of these four personality types, so if you can develop the skill to identify how other people communicate, then you can better connect with those who are different than you. You do this by modifying your own communication style when you sense that it will help you connect with someone.

According to Jung, the four personality types are: sensation, intuition, feeling, and thinking. Each personality type experiences the world differently, and we communicate based on our interests, needs, values, and motivation.

Since many of the significant challenges that a new business owner will need to address are based on interacting with people, it is important that you as a business owner do a self-assessment. You can choose to take a Myers-Briggs test, or you can use any similar test that will help you understand your own communication style. One benefit of the Myers-Briggs is that you'll measure your personality on a scale—it's not necessarily a one-or-the-other result. We have taken the Myers-Briggs test on multiple occasions for different reasons over the years, and the results were always enlightening. We have learned a lot about ourselves by comparing our results to how we see ourselves and how others see us too.

We've been surprised by our own results in the past. However, when we have shared them with close family members and friends to ask if the results were accurate, we were amazed to hear a resounding, "Are you kidding? That profile definitely fits you!

You can finish the Myers-Briggs test in under an hour, and the results can be quite informative, so we recommend that every would-be business owner take it before he begins any major undertaking. Since a new business owner is responsible for practically all facets of the business, he will be interacting with numerous people. Therefore, the owner will be well served to recognize his strengths and weaknesses and how best to approach other people whose personalities will differ during the course of conducting business.

As a SCORE counselor, I was introduced to the *Entrepreneur's Guide: Starting and Growing a Business in Pennsylvania ("Entrepreneur's Guide")*, published by the Center for Entrepreneurial Assistance in Harrisburg, PA. Unlike many government publications, I found this to be an excellent resource for new business owners. This guide discusses having the "right stuff" for being an entrepreneur. During the process of writing this book, I discovered that this guide is accessible online. You can find it at http://www.newpa.com/business/growing-business/download-guide.

Some of the personality traits of a potential small business owner that are discussed in the *Entrepreneur's Guide* include:

- Problem solving: Do you explore innovative ways to respond to opportunities?
- Goal oriented: Can you envision a desired outcome, as well as plan and implement the activities required to achieve the desired outcome?
- Self-confidence: Do you believe in your own ideas and abilities, and can you convey that belief to others?
- Risk taking: Can you abandon the status quo, explore options, and pursue opportunities?
- Decision making: Do you have the ability to make prudent choices even in a stressful environment?
- Persistence: Can you tenaciously pursue goals regardless of the energy and commitment required?
- Communication: Can you speak, listen and write effectively?
- Interpersonal relationships: Can you understand the wants and needs of others, as well as inspire them?
- Leadership: Can you direct others effectively and empower their performance?

The importance of these traits cannot be overstated. We suggest that after doing a self-assessment of the above traits you reread them several times so that they resonate within you. Write down specific situations in which you can envision prior experiences where you have successfully shown these traits.

The *Entrepreneur's Guide*, to its credit, lists these traits in its very first chapter. As a new business owner, you will be wearing several hats—you'll be responsible for numerous facets of your business including marketing, advertising, employee relationships, tax filings, financial statements, and a host of other matters. You will face numerous challenges and obstacles. Your results from the Myers-Briggs test will emphasize your strengths and reveal your weaknesses so that you can compare yourself honestly to the traits suggested in the *Entrepreneur's Guide*.

If you possess the traits suggested in the *Entrepreneur's Guide*, you will have the skill set to succeed. If you do not possess these specific entrepreneurial traits, it does not mean that you cannot succeed. It simply means that you know where you'll have to work harder. Likewise, even if you possess every one of the recommended skill sets, this does not mean that your business will be a financial success. We agree with the *Entrepreneur's Guide's* recommendation: if you lack any of these traits, then you need to take steps to build the missing traits or to strengthen the weak ones. Those weak traits can be strengthened by partnering with others or hiring employees who exemplify the positive traits that you lack. You can find a person with strong traits in a particular area and make them responsible for the job duties that require those skills. These persons can be family members, employees, consultants, and your team of trusted advisors. When I first took the Myers-Briggs test, I learned that my personality was not well suited for any job duties having to do with sales. (A truer observation could not have been made.) I have never wanted anything to do with sales, even before I took that initial test. However, my career path eventually changed, and I was required to become more involved with sales and marketing myself. Over time, as I got more involved with marketing, I became more comfortable with the personality traits needed to become a good salesman. Today, I find that a large part of our business is selling our expertise, and that I am actually quite good at it. I share this with you to highlight that all of us have the ability to turn our weaknesses into strengths.

CHAPTER 4

What Are The Odds Of Your New Business Being Successful?

There is a quote by the "great philosopher," Yogi Berra: "When you come to a fork in the road—take it!" While that may not initially make sense beyond its humorous viewpoint, there is in fact some deeper meaning in the statement. When we're not sure which path to take, we try our best to take both. After a lot of struggle, we find that we don't get very far down either one. Many small business owners find themselves in the same spot, because they use Yogi Berra's recommendation as their overall business strategy. This brings to mind another truism: "If you don't know where you are going, you will surely get there."

Just to let you know how serious the error of not having a clear path is, let's look at another truism for potential business owners:

More than half of new businesses fail within the first five years. [*]

And it doesn't get any easier as the years go on: Using U.S. government data, Mr. Scott Shane, a Professor of Economics at Case Western Reserve University, graphed the start-up survival rate from 0 to 16 years. The graph shows that two-thirds of new businesses fail within the first 10

[*] Scott Shane, Dec. 17, 2012. "Start Up Failure Rates: The Definitive Numbers" http://smallbiztrends.com/2012/12/start-up-failure-rates-the-definitive-numbers.html)

years, and in fact, only a quarter of small businesses remained after 16 years.

Based on our firm's interviews with small business owners who have decided to close their front doors after years 6 to 10, many reported that they did so because they came to the realization that they had erroneously assumed that owning their own businesses was tantamount to being financially successful. In other words, these small-business owners had assumed that owning a business would make them wealthy. While most of these businesses were profitable, when they considered the number of hours worked in their businesses, the profits were less than they would have earned as employees in traditional careers. When speaking with these owners, we found that most of them failed to work with a team of trusted advisors throughout their years in business; many of them attempted to do everything themselves or depended upon family members for guidance. In other words, many of them took the fork in the road without doing the work to choose a clear direction.

The point of these statistics and anecdotes is not to discourage you from starting your own business. To the contrary, we want to motivate you to understand the importance of starting your business the "right way." We want to help you prepare correctly to avoid the "small-business bone yard" after five or 10 years.

You will undoubtedly be investing a significant amount of time to start your business, and we know you may be making a sizable financial investment to get started. So isn't it prudent to take the necessary steps to protect your investment and know before starting your business where you will be in a few years?

We know some people will say: "These statistics are so bad! How can I ever succeed with such odds?" They might contemplate going into business and find themselves paralyzed with fear and uncertainty, never beginning their journey down the path to business success. And in other cases, just the opposite will happen when a person will begin a small business without considering the potential risks—he'll come to a fork in the road of his life and take it with little or no analysis. Don't be one of these persons! We want you to understand *why* you are getting into business for yourself. You may find a clue that you're starting a new business for the "wrong" reasons if you find that you're plunging forward in excitement without performing basic due diligence. If you don't have the patience and foresight to plan and make considered decisions *before* you begin, you may find over time that you don't have the commitment necessary for long-term success.

In either case, the end result is regret—regret about the path not taken or regret over taking the wrong path without consideration only to find financial pain and suffering. We believe that either of these scenarios can easily be avoided by taking the time to properly consider your business venture before choosing to begin.

We've already talked about your team of trusted advisors. We believe you'll increase your odds of success by surrounding yourself early with a good team of experienced professionals. These trusted advisors act as your mentors until such time that you have developed your own proficient level of expertise. Or in many cases, you may realize that the value they bring to the table is worth the fees they ask for their advice and guidance. Rather than relying solely upon words of encouragement from your family and friends, you should run your ideas past your trusted advisors who have years of experience working with start-up businesses.

In the next chapter, we'll explain how you can begin to build your team of advisors.

CHAPTER 5

How Do You Find Your Trusted Team of Advisors?

We believe your team of trusted advisors should consist of an experienced business attorney; a CPA/accountant who works with business owners and who is proficient with taxes (one of the largest expenses a business owner will incur); a business insurance agent or broker; and if you have a good relationship with your credit union or bank, then you should have a professional lender on your team. Once you have identified your team of advisors, meet with each of them early in the process. Share with them your vision and the steps that you will be taking, and ask if you can call on them for guidance or advice as you proceed through the process of starting your own business.

Many prospective business owners skip this very important step because they feel they must minimize fees as a start-up. But this thought process might be ill considered. Many of us would likely never consider replacing the brakes on our car by ourselves, because we realize the *value* of having an experienced auto mechanic perform this work. But entrepreneurs often make a similar mistake when they plan their start-up. They simply do not perceive that the legal and accounting professions provide value to business owners. Or, when an entrepreneur considers engaging such a professional, he is too fee conscious. It is easy to understand how a business owner can make this mistake, as advisors and other professionals often don't educate their customers about the need for professional tax, legal, financing, and business consulting services and how they will benefit the business owner.

For those who do realize there is value, some believe that it is a fungible commodity, meaning that the same value can be obtained by any means or from any person. Why pay a thousand dollars or more to hire an attorney to incorporate the business when you can go online and fill in a template for yourself for a couple of hundred dollars? Why engage an accountant when you can maintain your own books and records and file tax returns on TurboTax? The answers to these questions will be addressed later in this chapter.

When building a home or office building, a strong foundation is needed to ensure a long and safe life. If the structure has flaws or cracks, the life of the structure may be shortened or additional effort and capital will need to be invested to fix the cracks in the foundation. The same holds true when starting a business. As a new business owner, you must realize that professional help in your business will save you effort, time, and money. You are not an expert in law, accounting, taxes, or employee benefits. As advisors to businesses, we have seen countless business owners attempt to save money up front by doing these things themselves, only to discover later that the fees paid to correct mistakes were significantly more than if the proper steps had been taken from the start. This type of thinking reminds us of the Fram oil filter commercial: You can either pay a little now for an oil filter, or you will pay a lot later to rebuild your automobile's engine. We absolutely believe that you will find working with experienced professional advisors from the start is the best approach. First, you will have peace of mind knowing that your business is being managed properly; second, you will be able to devote your time to other facets of your business such as generating revenues and cash flows; and third, you will avoid even larger fees to these professionals (or worse, fines to the government!) to correct the inadvertent mistakes you made.

When the business owner asks around to find a good attorney or CPA, the typical response is to speak with your family, friends, and business associates and ask whom they use. The thinking is that if they are satisfied with their advisor, then you too will be satisfied. Unfortunately, our experience has been that business owners take this advice too literally and fail to perform any due diligence. They telephone or meet the recommended professional to ask if he or she is accepting new clients. If the fee arrangement seems reasonable, the advisor has been engaged.

The fact that your friend or business associate recommended his professional advisor should not be the sole criteria for selecting your trusted advisor. Your friend's business needs may be entirely different from your needs or your friend may be unaware of his advisor's deficiencies. Take a moment to remember Bernie Madoff—his clients were entirely word of mouth; and there are certainly others like him in the world. How many people lost large sums of money simply because they relied upon their friend's praise of Mr. Madoff? We refer to selecting your trusted advisor by relying solely upon a friend's recommendation as "blissful ignorance." You won't recognize your mistake until much later. It can be a very costly mistake which could have been avoided if you had done your due diligence. Since you are depending upon each advisor to safely navigate you through tax, legal or insurance storms, you cannot assume he is qualified to do so.

Over the years, we have seen business owners fail to take seriously the step of finding qualified advisors. We have heard business owners say that they do not need a CPA because their spouse took a bookkeeping or accounting course during her lifetime. One owner shared with us that he had hired his nephew who recently graduated from college as his accountant and thus had no need to engage a CPA. These business owners substantially increased their odds of failing because they did not understand the need to have a competent and experienced advisory team assist them.

We were working with a marketing person who shared with us his story. He had his longtime friend prepare his tax returns. He could not have been more pleased with the relationship they had. One day he was notified by the Internal Revenue Service (IRS) that he and his wife were being examined. This person was not concerned because he was confident that his longtime friend would settle the IRS audit without any problems. Unfortunately, this person learned the hard way (when he received a $60,000-plus assessment from the IRS) that his friend had been preparing their tax returns incorrectly all of those years. Not only did this person have a huge IRS bill to pay, but because of the ordeal, he lost his long-term friend also.

Let's look at it this way: If you were to have an appendectomy, you would likely ask your close circle of friends, family, and your family doctor for a referral. You'd meet with that doctor, review his credentials and experience, and likely even seek a second medical opinion. It is unlikely that the surgery would be performed by your spouse who took a medical course or by your nephew who just graduated from medical school. Why should the hiring of a trusted advisor for your business be any different?

Choosing your CPA or accountant, or any advisor, is not easy. As a CPA, I am a member of my state society of CPAs. The state societies and the American Institute of CPAs do an excellent job of marketing the CPA profession. If you have an accounting or tax problem, you are urged to call your local CPA for advice. While there is nothing wrong with this type of outreach by the professional societies from a marketing perspective, in our opinion it really does an injustice to the business owner or individual seeking tax or financial advice, because the organization's marketing leads one to believe that all CPAs are created equal. But they aren't. When all of these CPAs were in the classroom learning their profession, do you think that everyone was an A+ student? More likely, many students earned B's, C's, or even D grades in the classroom. How many of those candidates received a perfect score when they took the CPA exam? It's obvious that not all CPAs have the same level of experience and expertise, and yet when choosing their CPAs, many small-business owners do not take this into account. How many times have we heard a business owner tell us he chose us because we're conveniently located near his personal residence or place of business? Although geographic location can be a factor, it shouldn't be the first consideration when choosing a tax consultant. Unfortunately, this happens far too often.

The *most frequent first question* asked of us by a prospective business owner or individual taxpayer is "How much do you charge?" Although this is a valid question, we have to explain to the caller that he ought to be asking this question last rather than first. Instead of focusing on fees, the caller should be asking about our qualifications and experience. He should be grilling us about what services we can provide and how we can enable him to succeed. Once you are satisfied that you've found a competent and qualified CPA, you can then focus on the fee being charged.

For the business owner who hires advisors based only on how cheaply he can get them to work, there may come a time when he realizes just how expensive his choice really was.

We recently met with such a successful business owner who was looking for a CPA to review his accounting records and the business tax returns he had self-prepared. He hoped we could work on an "as needed basis," because although he had no accounting or tax background, he preferred to do everything himself to save on fees. He stated that he preferred to engage an accountant *only* when absolutely necessary, and that his former CPA had dropped him as a client to focus his practice on larger companies. His straight-forwardness was refreshing. As a way of background, the owner had used an online service to file his incorporation documents to create the company; but had he known what he knows today about limiting his legal liability, he told us he would have selected a limited liability company (LLC) rather than a corporation, and would have preferred not to be taxed as a C Corporation. During our meeting, we reviewed his accounting records, (which did not agree with his tax returns), and soon found that his tax returns were prepared incorrectly; furthermore, because of his selected legal entity, he was overpaying his taxes. While he may have saved a couple of thousand dollars when forming his company, he had paid dearly for his mistakes during the past five years in unnecessary taxes. Although we pointed these facts out, the client was still focused on not paying fees rather than the value he could receive by using our services. Thus, we had to inform him that we had no desire to serve him in such a limited capacity. Instead of focusing only on the limited services he requested, we suggested that he should focus on growing his business by networking with business associates, meeting with his clients to ensure that they were satisfied with his company's service, and asking clients to provide referrals. We suggested that we would be glad to perform his tax and accounting duties for him, which would free his time for activities that will grow his business. The value he would receive from our services would likely far exceed our fees; and with this in mind, we made the business owner a proposal to provide him with all of his tax and accounting needs. To his credit, the business owner recognized the value we could bring his business and he became a client of our firm. He realized that he needed to change his approach as he sought to expand his business operations. The insights that he gained were all because of a free consultation where we took the time to meet with him, showed him that his returns were improperly prepared, (which, by the way, can result in an IRS audit), and explained to him why he was overpaying his taxes. This business owner began to focus on the value he would receive rather than the fee he would need to pay. By allowing experts to prepare his tax returns, his anxiety would be replaced by peace of mind knowing that all returns were prepared properly, reducing his audit risk and freeing up more time for him to focus on the aspects of his business that truly needed his talents and attention.

Why did we share the above story with you? *We think it is vitally important that a business owner focus on the value of the services to be received and the expertise of the advisor, and not focus on the cost of those services.* Hopefully, the remainder of this chapter will provide you with some ideas as to how to find the best qualified accountant to meet your business needs.

What is the process to find a good accountant, Enrolled Agent (EA), or CPA? First, you need to have a basic understanding of the differences between these three appellations. For the purposes of this book, we took the liberty of using these names interchangeably. A CPA (certified public accountant) has passed a national examination administered by the State Board of Accountancy to show a level of proficiency in tax, accounting, auditing and legal matters. A CPA must be licensed to practice in a state and must meet the educational and ethics requirements of that state. A CPA is an accountant; however, an accountant is not necessarily a CPA. Most states do not have any type of licensing, educational, or ethical standards for a person to call himself an accountant. While there are many excellent accountants, a business owner will need to perform more extensive due diligence when hiring an accountant who is not also a CPA.

An Enrolled Agent (EA) is a federally-authorized tax practitioner who has technical expertise in the field of taxation and who is empowered by the U.S. Department of the Treasury to represent taxpayers before all administrative levels of the IRS for audits, collections, and appeals.

To become an Enrolled Agent, practitioners must pass a comprehensive examination, which covers all aspects of the Tax Code. Enrolled agent status is the highest credential awarded by the IRS.

Both CPAs & EAs are qualified to advise, represent and prepare tax returns for individuals, partnerships, corporations, estates, trusts and any entities with tax-reporting requirements.

But we must recognize that there are differences between the two. For example, an EA's primary specialty is in income taxes, while a CPA is trained to have a much broader focus. A CPA can be well versed in accounting, auditing, and income tax matters. Most CPAs eventually find a niche that lies within one of these. Since not all CPAs specialize in taxation, make sure yours does.

Due diligence on your tax advisor

As a first step, you need to meet with and interview at least three tax professionals to determine if they have the experience and expertise to advise you about your business. We believe it is most important that your accounting advisor be proficient about taxes for the reasons discussed below. Start by asking for referrals from your inner circle (family, business contacts, and friends) and by searching on the Internet and websites that review services. When you've found a potential advisor, carefully review the website to learn about the person's background, experience and credentials. You should check with the state licensing boards to see if there have been complaints filed against any CPAs you are considering.

If you're a small-business owner, taxes are important—aside from wages and cost of sales, they are the most significant expense you will likely incur. When a CPA is asked if he can handle taxes for a business, the answer is almost always an emphatic "Yes." But it can be hard to differentiate if your CPA is actually well qualified in this area. Many a CPA feels comfortable responding this way because he has the help of a software program to prepare individual and business tax returns. Even if he lacks the experience to understand the minutiae of tax law, he simply inputs the data into his tax preparation software program and hopes the return is properly prepared. However, when it comes to tax planning and strategic tax reduction, this type of CPA is clueless. In the end, it can often result in the business owner overpaying his taxes, reducing his cash flow needed to fund the business and making it more difficult for him to provide a quality life for his family.

Due diligence on attorneys or legal counsel

We have always been bothered that the CPA industry doesn't advocate more for specialization. While the previous example focused on the accounting profession, the same holds true when you are looking for an attorney. We believe it is important to include an attorney early in the process because the type of legal entity created, as well as the state in which the legal entity is formed, can have very significant asset protection implications. Not all legal entities and states provide the same limited liability protection. Because of the litigious society we live in, it is almost inevitable that you as a business owner will need the advice of legal counsel sometime in the future. You may need an attorney to collect unpaid receivables from a customer, respond to an employee or customer complaint, have a vendor or customer contract reviewed, modify legal documents, or respond to a legal suit, just to name a few examples. Why not develop that attorney relationship from the beginning when you are starting your business?

Due diligence on insurance agent or broker

When searching for your insurance agent or broker, you want to make sure that the agent has significant experience working with commercial entities and whose practice is not primarily related to residential home and auto policies. We have included in *Appendix A* examples of the various types of insurance policies you may need to consider as a business owner.

Most professionals will be glad to meet with a prospective client for a free consultation. If you have spent the time and effort to create a solid business plan (discussed in Chapter 8), then you will be intimately familiar with the issues that you and your business will be facing. So make sure the advisor you are meeting with is qualified to assist you with those issues. You need to make a list of questions to ask. You need to write down the answers during the consultation or immediately after the meeting so that you can compare your notes after meeting with each advisor. A sampling of such questions could possibly include:

- How long have you been practicing?
- How long have you been practicing at this location?
- What are your specialties or areas of expertise?
- What are your credentials?
- What types of clients do you handle?
- What are your professional affiliations?
- If I were to engage your firm, with whom would I be working? (If you will be working with someone other than the person across from the desk from you, you need to speak with that person).
- What has been your experience working with start-up companies?
- How many start-up companies have you worked with over the past year?
- How many clients do you have in my industry?
- What issues do you see in your practice that most new business owners face?
- How promptly do you return your client's phone calls?
- Please describe your tax/legal/insurance experience and expertise and how it may benefit me.
- Do you subscribe to any tax/legal/insurance research resources? Which ones do you read regularly?
- Do you have access to Internet research resources such as Lexis-Nexis or other academic and law databases?
- What distinguishes you from other local CPAs/attorneys/insurance brokers?
- You likely have identified a couple of industry or business issues that you have discovered during your due diligence. Ask the professional how he would handle these issues.
- If you like what you hear, then you should ask about fees. Remember that the fees paid should be commensurate with the value received.

During this process, you need to focus on how the professional responds to your questions. Is he annoyed? Is he evasive? Are his answers clear and definitive? Were his responses in layman language that you understood or did he quote code sections and used acronyms that meant nothing to you? Does he have a personality that makes you comfortable? Does he sound trustworthy?

After you met with the professional, did he follow-up to show his commitment to you and to tell you that he would like to have you as a client? Check out the testimonials on his website.

You need to realize during your consultation that the professional is also sizing up you as a possible client. Are you the kind of person he would feel comfortable having as a client? For example, during a recent consultation with a financial investment advisor who was searching for a CPA, the potential client shared with us his concern to find a CPA who does not charge much; and since he wasn't keen on keeping receipts or records with respect to his tax deductions, it was important to him that we would accept the estimated deductions he pulls from the sky. He informed us that research had shown that the chances of an IRS audit were not great, so he would play the audit lottery.

It was clear to us that under no circumstances would we ever enter into a client relationship with this person. We also felt sorry for the clients who might entrust their hard-earned retirement funds with this man who lacked a moral compass.

These examples and suggestions are just advice to get you started on your hunt. After you've met with this initial group of advisors, if you cannot a professional who is a perfect fit for your business, you should not settle. You should take the time to expand your search until you've found a team who will serve your interests well beyond the first 10 successful years of your business start-up.

CHAPTER 6

Do You Have A Viable Business?

Many a budding entrepreneur rushes in without sufficient planning and research. Either he immediately begins by creating his own business, or he purchases an existing business. Examples of rushing in would include applying for an employer identification number (EIN), signing a lease because you have found the "ideal location" and do not want to lose it, visiting banks without having created a business plan and asking for a loan that you'll use to buy inventory or purchase equipment, paying for a website and host services because you have "an idea for a business" but never take it any further than paying out money to create the website, or signing a contract to purchase an existing business or franchise without performing the necessary due diligence. Many people who want to start a business really have no clue as to where to start, so they're prone to doing whatever first comes to mind.

If you do not plan to start your own business from scratch, opting instead to buy an existing business or purchase a franchised business, *you still need to perform your due diligence before proceeding.* We will discuss some specifics of purchasing your own business or a franchise in Chapter 7. But it is important to keep in mind that purchasing an existing business or a franchise is no different than starting your own business with respect to the due diligence you must perform.

The very first and most important step you need to address is whether you have a viable business.

We believe that this question is the most important question that the new business owner must address, and it is often overlooked. Many a new business owner simply plunges into the business because it is something that he enjoys and wants to do, or because he assumes the product or service is needed. But these are not givens. Even if you have the greatest mousetrap ever invented, you must determine whether there is there a need for the product in the marketplace. Far too many new business owners suffer from what we call the "Field of Dreams" syndrome—"If I build it, they will come!" Although they are not building a baseball field in the cornfields of Iowa, they believe that by opening the doors to their business, customers will flock inside to purchase their product or service make them financially successful beyond their wildest dreams. If only it were so easy.

Our objective in discussing whether you have a viable business is to prevent you spending a significant amount of money in your business only to find that that the initial concept was flawed.

I met with one business owner who was struggling with his business. The competition in his geographic area was very high, which resulted in consumers looking at price as the determining factor. When we asked the owner why he had selected a location with so much competition nearby, he responded that he lived out of state and desired to live near his mother. Since he was not familiar with the area, he had asked his mother to find a location for his store. Had he the opportunity to go back in time, he realized that there were much better locations.

We had a client who was considering changing his family restaurant, which catered to an elderly crowd, to a sports bar because the young patrons who frequented the bar after work had suggested he should do so. When he looked at the local competition for a sports bar, he found none. To his credit, he did some research—he called us and asked us our thoughts. With some basic research on the Internet, we found that the demographics of the area where his restaurant was located simply were not suitable: roughly 50 percent of the residents within a 25-mile radius of his restaurant were over the age of 70. This fact not only explained why most of his customers were elderly, but also explained why there were no sport bars operating in his geographic area.

The aforementioned *Entrepreneur's Guide* (mentioned in Chapter 3) suggests 10 questions for the business owner to consider. We have cherry picked some of the questions we believe are the most important, and we have paraphrased these questions below along with our own comments and observations.

1. **Does the product or service satisfy the needs of the customer, or simply the desire of the business owner?** Just because you have a hobby or skill and love doing what you are doing, this does not automatically translate into a product (or service) that is desired by the buying public. You must determine the probable size of the market for your product.

2. **Does the product you offer have an identifiable advantage over the competition?** John Nelson, with whom I have co-mentored at SCORE and who has a great marketing background, often tells business owners of the importance of a "USP." The USP is the unique selling (or value) proposition of the business. It does not matter whether the business owner perceives that he has a USP—but **it is very important that the *buyer* perceives a USP**. Saying that you will provide the customer with quality service is not a legitimate USP. Every business says that it will deliver quality service. You need to identify what separates your business from your competitors in the eyes of the consumer.

3. **Can the quality of the product be maintained at a level that encourages buyers to return to buy?** When I read this, I think of McDonalds. McDonalds wants its buyers to know, regardless of the region or country in which a hamburger and fries are purchased, that the buyer's expectation of quality and consistency will be totally satisfied. When our daughter visited Moscow during the Cold War years, though she didn't particularly desire a McDonalds' hamburger in the USA, she found it very attractive in Moscow because of the confidence she had in her expectations as to how the food would taste.

4. **Are there a sufficient number of customers in the market to support another competitor?** While the market size was sufficient for the first business owner and perhaps the next few owners, there comes a point where the market becomes saturated and there are not enough buyers to sustain all of the businesses that offer the same product, especially one lacking a USP. We have seen this in the coffee business. A few years ago, we observed Starbucks as it hit the East Coast. Pretty soon, there seemed to be a Starbucks on every street corner. Then other franchises and coffee houses opened. Tea shops opened. At that point, Starbucks began to close some of its stores. This is part of the business cycle, and you need to understand it for your industry and the competition that you will face.

5. **Is the product compatible with existing beliefs, attitudes and buying habits of prospective customers?** I remember when video stores that rented VHS and Betamax tapes were the rage. These were new products that met the needs of the consumer at that time, but within 15 years they gave way to DVD and Blu-ray discs. Today, consumers don't want to pick up and return videos during business hours. They don't want to be told that the video they want to see tonight will not be available until it is returned next Wednesday. Today, the consumer wants to select the video of choice at the time most convenient to them, to know that the video is instantly available, and to have the choice of watching that video on a Smartphone, tablet, personal computer, or TV. How many video stores are still in existence today? How many drive-in theatres exist today?

6. **Is the price of the product within an affordable range for the intended target market?** While you may have a better product, is the price of your product comparable to existing products on the market? If your product is priced higher, will the consumer see the increased value of your product and be willing to pay a premium? If your product is priced higher than others in the market because of its cost and there is no

additional perceived value to your product, will you be able to reduce the selling price of your product and its production cost to remain price competitive?

Okay, the above are very important questions, but how does one find the answers to these questions?

7. The answer is quite simple; but the task is not. **You need to do RESEARCH, RESEARCH and more RESEARCH.** One of the technical terms used is that you must do your **due diligence**. By thoroughly researching your new business concept, you will become an expert in your industry and your chances of succeeding will significantly improve. You will exponentially improve the odds that you will not be included in the over 50 percent of new business failures within the first five years. You will find peace of mind as your life will be less stressful moving forward.

While all of the research tools at your disposition are too numerous to discuss, we believe it is important that you at least be aware of the following primary and secondary research resources. Primary research involves your first-hand collection of data and information. It can include speaking with collaborators or competitors in the industry, taking surveys, and using your powers of observation to determine traffic counts and seasonal influences on your business. Secondary research involves collecting data that has already been compiled by others. This usually consists of information that is found in printed materials. We have found that using secondary sources often provides more accurate data, is less time-consuming, and may be less biased than your first-hand research, which may be tainted with your hope or expectation for a favorable result.

Trade Associations: Most industries have local, regional, and national trade associations. The cost to join an industry trade association is relatively inexpensive. The benefits of joining a trade association are numerous. First, you will likely obtain a list of association members and their contact information. Second, many industries publish general facts about their industries, such as average sales revenues, labor cost as a percentage of revenues, gross profit margins, net profit margins, etc.—you get the picture. Third, there are the regional and annual meetings where members of the trade association gather for educational discussions, presentations; and they get the opportunity to network with others within the trade. Is there a better source to gather information about an industry than from its association and other business owners in that industry?

Professional Associations: There are various associations that publish financial facts about certain industries. For example, the Risk Management Association (RMA) is a professional association whose sole purpose is to advance sound risk principles in the financial services industry. If you are thinking of entering some type of financial services industry, the RMA would be a good resource. The RMA also has a publication that analyzes various business metrics. You should see if it includes your industry in its guidebook. Business metrics are the factors that drive the economics of the business. If you understand the metrics of your business and can improve those metrics in your own business operation, then you are generating additional cash flows.

Trade Shows and Conventions: Check the local and various state convention centers to see if your industry will be holding a convention there. If you are a member of the trade association, those convention meetings will be readily available to you. If you find that your industry will be having a convention and you are not a member of that trade association, contact the convention center about whether the public is invited to intend or if the convention is limited to members. If attendance is limited to the latter, you need to become a member or make friends with a member to attend as a guest.

Securities and Exchange Commission (SEC): Publicly-held companies (large companies with stockholders) are required to file Form 10-K with the SEC, and they must send their shareholders an annual report. Of the two documents, we prefer the 10-K, which contains significantly more detailed information than the annual report. Why would you want to look at a public-held company's filings if you just want to be a small business owner? Form 10-K will show the financial results of that business for the past several years. These details give you vital information about the trend of your industry. Is the business growing, declining, or going nowhere? What is the percentage of labor costs to revenues? What is the company's gross profit margin and net profit margin? If the company is being sued, discover why and by whom. Litigation and pending suits may alert you to issues you may have initially overlooked. If any lawsuits relate to liability claims, have you discussed these suits with *your* insurance broker and attorney to ensure that you are adequately insured? If you are considering paying to become a franchisee, are any of the suits are being brought by other franchisees? You need to understand these suits, as they may affect your business operations. The concerns of existing franchisees could become yours. How healthy is the parent company? How many new store locations are being opened each year? While the company's revenues are growing annually, is this revenue growth coming from existing or new locations? A review of several publicly-traded companies' Form 10-K and annual reports will give you a greater insight to industry trends. This may be an appropriate time to get a qualified and competent accountant to analyze these public filings and provide you with a trend analysis and summary of the key benchmarks for your industry. If litigation is an issue for this business or industry, consult with your legal counsel to understand the potential impact upon your business.

Franchisors: Are there franchisors in this industry? If so, contact them. While you may not be currently interested in franchising, remember that you are now performing research on your industry and need to become an expert in it. If there is a resource available, you should use it. A franchisor provides much information about the costs its franchisees can expect to incur. You may be able to speak with current franchisees about the challenges they have faced, the profitability of the business, cash flows, and unexpected costs. Another valuable resource is ex-franchisees. Call them and ask why they are ex-franchisees. Much valuable information can be gained from an ex-franchisee. You do not want to make the same mistakes they made. If the ex-franchisee tells you that they signed a gag order with the franchisor that prevents them sharing why they are no longer a franchisee, try and be creative and ask about the challenges they faced as a franchisee.

Internet Searches: The Internet is a great resource to learn more about the challenges facing an industry. Large investment firms often make their research reports about an industry or a company (in your industry) available on the Internet. You can read these research reports to see what opportunities and challenges the research analyst has identified and if you need to consider these in your analysis. Many public libraries or local universities offer public access to institutional and government databases. You could schedule an appointment with a research librarian, who will guide you through the process of accessing resources in your subject area.

Business Research Librarian: Contact your local business research librarian and make an appointment to discuss what your research project is and how the librarian may assist you. Libraries have a wealth of informational resources to which they subscribe. The librarian should be able to assist you in identifying the number of similar businesses as yours within a 5-mile, 10-mile and 15-mile radius of your planned location. Record the contact information and addresses of these businesses and then visit them to see what services they offer. Just to name a few considerations—look at their pricing, hours of operation, and qualifications. Try to determine what are their USPs (did you remember that this is your unique selling proposition?).

Ask the librarian if he or she can suggest any industry guidebooks, governmental agencies, or annual reports of public companies (and their 10-K forms) that may be able to assist you. Find out if there are any online resources the library has that you may be able to access from your home computer.

Additional resources that the research librarian is likely to be familiar with include the local Chamber of Commerce, local Small Business Association chapters, the U.S. Small Business Association, local colleges and universities that may have research or policy initiatives related to your industry, brokerage house reports on your industry, demographic information from the U.S. Census Bureau, and key wage information from your state and the U.S. Department of Labor. Hopefully this short list will illustrate just a few of the vast numbers of research materials available to you through the library.

Non-Competitors: You need to speak with people who are already in the business to learn more about the challenges and opportunities they have experienced. Armed with lists of members from related trade associations, and names of out-of-state businesses obtained from your business research librarian, contact business owners in states where your new business would not be considered a threat. Some people just like to talk, especially about themselves. If you call business owners outside of your region, where the existing business owner would not consider you a competitor, you can learn key business factors such as: the amount of revenues in that business' early years, mistakes they made that you could avoid, industry challenges, seasonality, the ideal customer profile, what constitutes the ideal business location, peak business hours for staffing, and a host of other answers that only a similar business operator could offer you.

Competitors: Is the number of competitors increasing, decreasing, or is the market stable? Once you understand how your competition is trending, you can explore the "Whys." First, you will need to identify your competitors, both direct and indirect.

For example, if you are in the automobile repair industry, your direct competitors are other auto repair shops. Indirect competitors are shops that sell automobile parts for the do-it-yourselfers, stores that only sell tires and batteries, and oil change franchises, to name three.

You will eventually be in the position where you can visit the local competition. You are visiting these sites to observe. Some of you may find this step uncomfortable, as it is in practice a kind of spying. You need to remember that you are making a major life decision, and you want to know everything there is about other businesses in your industry, especially in your local market. If you have done your research using the research resources discussed in this chapter, then by now you will have a very detailed list of items that you can observe and record when visiting the local competition.

Items to consider during your visit include:

- What are their business hours?
- What are the credentials of their key employees?
- What products and services are offered?
- How does the competition price their products and services? How does that pricing compare to your pricing model?
- How do they treat their customers? Do they make their customers feel special, or do they take them for granted?
- Are their unique selling propositions (USPs) obvious? If not, go ahead and ask them the question "If I were to become

a customer of yours, what makes you different from your competitors?" Ask yourself, "How does their USP compare to yours?"

- What about signage? Advertising? What kinds of literature or brochures are available?
- Location?
- What does the competition do best? Do they have any weaknesses you think you could improve upon? Check out the competition's website. Is it just an online billboard, or is the website functional for the customer? Does the website grab the attention of the viewer?

Vendors: If you can make contact with key vendors (suppliers) that you will also need to use, be sure to speak with them now. Vendors are a great resource of information. As existing business owners know, speaking with vendors is a great way to learn how your competition is doing. If a business is slowing down and the business is decreasing its orders for supplies, the vendor will know first. If several businesses are decreasing their orders, perhaps the industry is slowing. If you are looking to hire, these vendors know which businesses are having problems and where you may find good employees looking for a change of employment.

Armed with all of your research, you can now address the central questions of your due diligence. Do you have a viable business? Is there a need for the product or service? Is the market large enough to provide you with a sufficient number of customers to cover your expenses and return a reasonable profit? What will your USP be?

As you compile all of this research material, it is very important that you carefully reference where you found the information you are depending upon for your business plan's assumptions. Eventually, these will be scrutinized. If a lender or investor challenges one of your assumptions, you want a system in place that gives you the ability to identify where you found the source of the data so that it stands up to any scrutiny.

Assuming that you have assured yourself and your trusted advisors that you have a viable business concept, how do you start or acquire that business? We'll discuss some options in the next chapter.

CHAPTER 7

Should You Start Your Own Business, Purchase An Existing Business Or Become A Franchisee?

I n this chapter, we will discuss purchasing an existing business or becoming a franchisee. Regardless of how you begin your business, the chapters to follow will guide you through the process of deciding how best to proceed and which of these three options is best for you.

If you start your own business, the advantage is that you are creating your own business model. There are no pre-existing conditions, restraints, or rules or policies to follow. But there will be a myriad of obstacles and issues that you will need to address as you write your business plan. These include finding customers, developing pricing structures, marketing strategies, and securing financing, just to name a few. Of the three options to become a business owner—start your own, buy an existing business, or become a franchisee—we believe based on our experiences as CPAs that most entrepreneurs prefer to start their own business from scratch.

Purchasing an existing business may better fit your needs. Some new business owners simply look for a business that is for sale, any business. Some people read the classified ads for business opportunities and contact the seller directly. Others meet with a business broker to inquire about businesses they are representing that are listed for sale. The first— and often, sadly, the only—question asked of the broker is: "What do you have available for sale?"

Be careful about this approach. You need to remember that unless you engage (hire) the business broker and pay him a fee, this broker has been retained by the *owner of the business* to sell the business. As such, the broker is acting in the best interests of the seller (and not your own best interests as the buyer).

You need to explore the reasons why the business is being sold. These could be numerous, and you may never know the true reason a business in being sold. The owner may have had a very successful business, and now he is simply ready to retire and live the American Dream. On the other hand, the business owner may be in either the first or second five-year cycle of the business, as described earlier in this book, and now he hopes to be saved from his own folly before things turn really bad.

One of our clients came to the realization that as a small business he could not compete against larger national companies. The owner realized that the large firms, to obtain market share, would simply underprice him. His business offered a commodity service, and it did not have a unique selling proposition. While the larger firms had the financial resources to sustain themselves for a long period of time by slashing their prices, our client's business was financed with a second mortgage on his primary residence. If our client could not sustain the current cash flow stream, he justifiably feared that his family could lose their home. What was our client's purported reason for selling the business? "After building a very successful business over the past five years, the owner desired to spend more time with his aging parents, who were in ill health."

Thus, while it is important to explore the reasons why the seller is selling, you need to understand that you as the buyer cannot rely upon those representations. *Caveat emptor*—let the buyer beware. The same goes for the sales broker. With respect to the business, he is representing the seller, and his commission is generally a percentage of the sales price. Thus, the higher the sales price, the happier both the seller and broker will be. The broker's obligation with respect to the buyer is to make sure that you, the buyer, are financially qualified to purchase the business. He is not under any obligation to make sure that you will make money after you purchase the business. That is your sole responsibility.

The seller of a business often believes that his business is worth far more than it is actually worth. Sellers will always base valuation on emotions rather than a standard valuation of the business. A good business broker will work with the seller to show him the true value of the business. The broker may base his valuation on other similar businesses that have sold recently. If the business owner insists that his business is worth far more than the value recommended by the broker, some brokers will not work with the seller, because at the owner's asking price there is little chance of success of selling the business. Meanwhile, the broker will be out-of-pocket for his costs and time to market a business that likely will not sell. In such cases, the broker may recommend that a valuation study be completed to determine the nominal value of the business.

A valuation study is done by a business valuation firm employing certified appraisers. The value of a business is primarily determined by analyzing the free cash flows from that business over the past several years, then projecting those cash flows into the future. In addition to revenue flow, the valuation study will take into account trends and standards of the industry and compare the business to those. Other points are also reviewed, such as the competitiveness of the industry, along with ease of entry and exit from the industry, and the unique selling propositions the business offers (if any). Finally the assets and equity of the business are considered. Since some of the assets of an existing business are intangible, consisting of the value of an existing customer base and the goodwill of the business and the personal goodwill of the owner, there can be much discretional judgment as to the value of those assets. Thus, the certified valuation expert will value the business using different market methodologies and will provide a range of values in their final report. As with any financial analysis, the results are directly related to the assumptions they're based upon. However, the valuation company will usually work with the seller to show the greatest value allowed by the standards to which the appraiser must abide.

Therefore, if you as a buyer are told by the seller or broker that they've commissioned an "independent valuation study" showing that the value of the business is "X" dollars, your trusted accountant should help you analyze that valuation study to determine if you agree with the assumptions on which it is based.

What is the true market value of a business? In truth, this is a very difficult number to pin down. While market valuations show the expected fair market value, the actual market value is what a willing buyer will pay to a willing seller. If you, the buyer, overpay for the business, you can be assured that the broker and seller will not object. On the other hand, if you are not willing to pay the price determined by the valuation report, but the seller is willing to accept $25,000 less than that, then the amount you paid is the fair value of that business.

There is an adage in real estate that the amount of money you make on the sale of a property is largely determined by what you paid when the property was purchased, not by the price for which it is sold. The same holds true for the purchase of an existing business. If you overpay for the business, you may never have a financially viable business. Or at best, the amount you've overpaid for the business will negatively impact your cash flows and profits for some time. But if you pay a fair and reasonable price for the business, you will enjoy the financial rewards of owning the business.

We sometimes have a new client share with us the following complaint: "I don't understand what I am doing wrong. I purchased a new business and my results are nowhere near what the seller told me I could expect. Can you help me?" In most cases, unfortunately, we cannot. In these situations, the client relied solely upon the representations of the seller when he purchased the business. In some cases these representations may have been the purported income tax returns of the business. But the income tax returns shown by the seller to the buyer must be representative of the business, right?

We were asked by a friend of the firm to meet with his fiancée, who had purchased a business about a year earlier in a very trendy neighborhood but was now having severe cash flow problems. The buyer was struggling financially and could not understand why the business was doing so much worse than when the seller had been running it. We were familiar with this location and we knew that the foot traffic at this retail operation should have been quite significant. When we asked to see the financial statements that the seller had provided so that we could compare them with the actual results, we were told that the fiancée had only been shown the seller's tax returns. This is not uncommon with small businesses, which are often run in such a way that they do not have financial statements. The buyer also shared that the seller had said with a wink and a smile that the tax returns may have "inadvertently" failed to report all of the revenues earned from cash sales and may have "inadvertently" included some personal expenses. This kind of dodgy communication by the seller led the buyer to believe that the business was more profitable than it appeared on the seller's tax returns. When we asked to see the tax returns that the buyer had received and reviewed, we were told that the seller did not provide copies due to the confidential nature of these returns. When we asked if the buyer had ever confirmed the information shown on the tax returns with the IRS, the couple was embarrassed to say that no independent verification had ever been made. They had simply assumed that the seller had shown them his actual tax returns. In this case, the buyer had failed in performing due diligence on the business and its revenue flows.

Most buyers would not have purchased a used car from that same seller relying solely upon such representations. A critical buyer would have at least taken the car for a test drive, or had his mechanic inspect the car for inconsistencies or major problems. Yet, this couple had purchased a business for far more money than they would have spent on any used car—and they had done it without the proper due diligence. If only she had asked a CPA to verify the tax return information, the buyer could have avoided much heartache and financial grief. We will later discuss these basic aspects of due diligence.

You've heard it said a million times: "Cash is king!" The same is doubly true when it comes to a small business. Every business owner must know and understand the operation's cash flows. It is amazing how many buyers do not perform even the most basic cash flow analysis. They look at the seller's representations, see that the reported revenues exceeded the reported expenses, and they are ready to fork over tens of thousands of dollars or more for the business. Not only do some buyers automatically accept the seller's representations, but they often compound the problem by making all kinds of assumptions about how to increase revenues, decrease operating expenses, and basically do much better than the previous owner did. It is easy to get caught up in a sense of euphoria that buying an existing business will be an easy way to make money. Without doing sufficient due diligence to fully understand the metrics of the business, there is much folly associated with the buyer's belief that he can run the business better than the seller without any prior experience in the business or industry.

Buying of a franchise may be of interest to you. In this section, we'll touch upon some of the considerations related to becoming a franchisee. There are many advantages to operating a franchise business. For example, the franchisor has already developed operating plans and marketing strategies, and the company provides you with training as to how to effectively use those systems. The franchise may be a nationally known firm, which means your business will have instant name recognition and credibility. The franchise will have its own marketing plan, and centrally produced advertising on television or radio of a higher quality and lower cost than you could do yourself. The franchise's real estate department will work with you to find an ideal location. This is what is typically referred to as a turn-key operation. Ideally, the business owner simply needs to turn the key in the front door and his business is up and running and ready for customers. In our CPA practice, we have worked with many franchisees over the years. At one time, we were franchisees ourselves. The first question we suggest that you ask yourself is whether you can religiously follow, without deviation, the procedures set by the franchisor for your operations. Some franchises control every aspect of the business, which are outlined in their uniform procedures manual. This means that the products offered, hours of operation, product displays, promotions—everything is controlled by the franchisor. If you are a person who wants to do your own thing and not follow the rules of corporate headquarters, then a franchise likely is not a good fit for you, or you will need to find a franchise that allows the franchisee a freer hand.

The success of most franchises is based on the concept that regardless of which store location you visit in any state, you can expect and will receive the same product and customer service. We mentioned this in an earlier chapter when we discussed the expectation of McDonalds' customers.

Some prospective franchisees think that owning a franchise is a sure way to financial success because they know that hundreds or thousands of franchised stores are operating. With so many stores operating, it must be a safe investment to make. When we have spoken to franchisees over the years, it was surprising how many of them shared with us that, while the franchise was highly successful for the franchisor, it was not for the franchisee.

When I was attending Villanova University to earn my master's in tax degree, I took a tax shelter course. The course was taught by Francis Grey, a tax partner with one of the Big-Eight accounting firms, Coopers & Lybrand, my employer at that time. (Today, this company is known as PricewaterhouseCoopers). During the first class, Mr. Grey said he was going to share with us one of the questions that would be on the final exam. The test question would provide a very detailed summary about a firm promoting a tax shelter as an investment for sale to individual investors. The test question would include numerous facts and figures about the tax shelter and what the investors of the shelter could expect in return for their monetary investment. After outlining all this information, the exam question would ask: "Is this tax shelter a good investment?"

Mr. Grey said that some students in our class would take 45 minutes to write a very elaborate answer detailing why the tax shelter would or would not be a good investment for the investor. He said that some students would also detail whether the tax shelter would be a good product for the tax shelter promoter as well. But all that would be unnecessary. In fact, Mr. Grey said, the simple answer was "Yes, the tax shelter is a good investment for *someone*; otherwise it would not have been brought to market." This answer would be considered 100 percent correct, and it should only take a few seconds to answer. Rather than spend 45 minutes on this question, Mr. Grey's advice was to move on to the next question.

Mr. Grey, who was very active with working with promoters of tax shelters and their clients who invested in them, told our class that the promoter of the tax shelter was bringing it to market because it would make money *for the promoter*. In fact, the promoter was going to make lots of money, which made it a fine deal for him regardless of the investor's return on investment. Thus, it was a good tax shelter for *someone*. I have always remembered this lesson when I hear prospective franchisees say that the business opportunity must be a good investment or else the franchisor would not be offering new locations to franchisees. The fact that the franchisor makes money does not necessarily mean that the franchisee will make money.

We're not trying to sound cynical. We know that there have been many successful franchised businesses, but we've also seen several franchise opportunities that were not successful. As stated above, while the franchisor may find a franchise to be a good investment, this does not necessarily translate into the franchisee making a good investment. The prospective franchisee must do his due diligence. Just to add to the discussion, we'd like to cite a recent article found on www.inc.com that discusses a Small Business Administration study showing the success rate of various franchise opportunities. Of these companies, the Pro Golf franchise had a failure rate of almost 70%, Carvel Ice Cream had a failure rate of 48%, and Blockbuster Video had a failure rate of 37.5% (and of course, is now in bankruptcy).

Whether you are considering buying an existing business or a franchise, we strongly recommend that the buyer create a trusted team of advisors, including at least a business attorney and an accountant. This team can develop a timeline of items that the buyer needs to address during the process of due diligence. For the entrepreneur who is considering buying a franchise, the first item that all parties will likely want to review is the Uniform Franchise Offering Circular.

Likewise, the prospective buyer needs to have the final sales agreement and, if applicable, the franchise agreement, reviewed by an attorney who specializes in these fields. Also, an expert needs to help with analyzing the cash flows from the business, discussing legal and tax entity structures, the structure for financing the purchase of the business, asset protection strategies, formulating a business plan based on reasonable and supportable assumptions, checking with the state Attorney General's office to see if complaints have been filed against the franchise, learning as much about the business and the industry as possible, and numerous other items.

In summary, it makes little difference whether you are starting your own business, buying an existing business, or buying a franchise. In all cases, **you must do your due diligence** and write a business plan regardless of how the business is being acquired.

CHAPTER 8

What Is a Business Plan?

A business plan is a document that captures your research (due diligence) and puts it down on paper. It needs to be done in an orderly fashion so that it will be readily understood by you, your trusted advisors, and others who may have a need to see the business plan, such as a lender. It is a "living" document, and as such, it is not set in stone. As the entrepreneur learns more about his business while performing due diligence, and as the business matures from the spark of an idea to the actual start-up to a growing company, this business plan needs to be flexible so that it can likewise adapt to provide continuing guidance to the business owner. In other words, once you have written the business plan, you will undoubtedly revise it continually as your business develops. These changes might stem from changes in economic conditions, your experience with actual sales and expenses versus earlier projections of those items, or a host of other market factors.

You have undoubtedly been told that your business needs a budget. Rather than starting your annual budget each year from scratch, why not use your business plan as the foundation for your budget? What we are saying is that although you will be spending a significant amount of time creating your business plan, if used properly, and revised when needed rather than merely stuffing it in a desk drawer when it is completed, it will guide you for many years.

It is not feasible to adequately discuss in detail all of the components of a good business plan in a single chapter; an entire book could be written on this subject. However, this chapter will explain how your business plan can be the balancing factor between a successful business and a "barely hanging together" business. By the time you've read this chapter, you'll understand the basic elements of the business plan and how you can begin to write it.

Most prospective business owners find the writing of a business plan to be a monumental and forbidding task. Therefore, many potential entrepreneurs tend to ignore it. It's not that they don't want to write a business plan, but they do not have the background and experience to know how to structure it, what to put into it, and how it will benefit their start-up plans. Accordingly, many people prefer to skip this task's demanding requirements. Instead, they open their doors for business with a blind reliance on the "Field of Dreams" syndrome. They'll think to themselves, "We're open for business. Now I only have to wait for the customers to come into the store and purchase my product; soon I'll have a successful business." Unfortunately, they'll soon find that it's not enough to build it and expect the crowds to come.

Aside from not researching to determine if you actually have a viable business concept, we believe the single major mistake made by most prospective business owners is not writing a business plan.

If you want a successful business, you need to have a sound business plan. We wish we could tell you that a business plan is such an easy task that it can be written in less than an hour. Unfortunately, that is not the case. If your goal is to secure financing to build or purchase a successful business, you will find that writing a business plan will require a significant amount of time and hard work. But do not be disheartened by this prospect! In our personal experiences with helping entrepreneurs with their business plans, we've found that the process of creating a business plan is exciting and contagious—once you get started learning more about your industry, considering different locations, evaluating your competition, building the pricing structure of your product or service, and working on the various other factors involved with the writing of a business plan. Your enthusiasm and desire will only grow as you become an expert in your industry. It's like learning to play golf or tennis. It's not easy to learn the basics of the sport—it demands much of your time and your commitment. However, as you slowly become more proficient, your interest in the sport grows, and you want to spend more time practicing so that you can become even better!

We believe that the main reason an owner will skirt the writing of a business plan is that he does not know where to start. If the owner did not do his due diligence and research, the information that is so vital to the business plan is not available and it makes writing the business plan so much more difficult.

Where to start: If you don't know where to start to write a business plan, there are numerous resources available to assist you. Again, there is the local business research librarian. You can do Internet searches on Google and other search engines and find various templates for business plans. Your local bookstore and library will have shelves of books on how to write a business plan. You should also contact your local SCORE office and ask for a mentor to assist you in learning how to write a business plan. As mentioned earlier, SCORE is part of the U.S. Small Business Association and can be found at www.sba.gov. Once you are on the SBA website, click on the Local Assistance menu option to find your local SCORE office. While the SCORE mentor will not write your business plan for you, the mentor will provide you with guidance, answer your questions, and give you feedback about the effectiveness of your business plan. The mentoring is a free service that you can avail yourself of as many times as needed, and it is available to both start-ups and to more mature businesses. SCORE also has sample business plans on its website that can easily be downloaded and adapted for your usage.

While business plans are commonly associated with start-ups, it would be an excellent idea if even established businesses had a business plan to help guide them. The mature business owner needs to continuously and periodically review his business plan. Let's face it. We live in a consumer world that is constantly changing. If the business owner is going to survive in a world where the consumer's needs are constantly changing, the business plan is a great tool to utilize to monitor the changes you are making to your business and the financial results of those changes.

There are actually two components of a good business plan. There is the written verbiage, which includes such items as your mission statement, executive summary, identifying your target market, your marketing plan, insurance, human resources, and various other narratives. The second component of a business plan is the projections of cash flows from the business. The financial part of the business plan will include a monthly projection of revenues and expenses for at least the greater of the first 12 months or when the business's cash flows become positive, and then an annual projection for the succeeding four years.

As a mentor of the Chester County SCORE chapter, I have often recommended to business owners to use the business plan templates on the SCORE website. SCORE offers a sample Word document for the written portion of the plan and an Excel worksheet for the financial projections so that you can "grind the numbers". Both of these templates are valuable resources that will jump-start the writing of the business plan and make the writing of the business plan much easier to complete. Again, avail yourself of a SCORE mentor to critique your business plan as you work on it and to provide you with suggestions for those items of the plan that you may find challenging.

If you do not feel comfortable writing a business plan, or you feel that your time could be better spent elsewhere, inquire if a member of your trusted team of advisors will assist you with the writing of the plan or doing some of the research needed for the plan.

Perhaps it is because I am a CPA and an accountant that I find the financial projections, and not the narrative, to be the most important component of an effective and compelling business plan. I read the business plan as I would read the annual report of a public traded company reporting its financial results to its shareholders. I initially ignore the chief executive officer's (CEO) message to the shareholders about how the business is doing and dive right into the numbers (the financial statements and footnotes of the annual report). I want to see how I think the business is doing based on the financial statements included in the annual report or Form 10-K rather than hearing how the business is doing looking through the rose-tinted eyeglasses of the CEO in his message to the shareholders. So when I am handed a business plan, I put aside the written part and go directly to the financial projections. Earlier in the book I mentioned the conspicuously credulous business plan that projected $2 million in revenues per month for the entire 24-month period of the business plan. Once I saw those numbers, I immediately realized that the owner had not done his due diligence. Even assuming that the first month revenues could be $2 million, there is no way that the business could operate with a constant revenue stream for 24 consecutive months. Any bank lender looking at those financial projections would have come very quickly to the same conclusion. The business owner would have lost his credibility with the lender in the opening minutes of the meeting to request a business loan. This was a clear case where the owner merely inserted his assumptions into the plan with no research supporting his assumptions.

Most business owners start with the written portion of the plan. We disagree with that approach and we ourselves would find writing a business plan very difficult if we were to start there. Think about it. The written portion of the plan discusses the industry, how you will differentiate yourself from your competition, pricing, marketing strategies, etc. It also discusses your cash flows and profitability. How do you write about all of this without having the data to support your claims? **We recommend to our clients that they do not even attempt the written portion of a business plan until the financial projections are completed and they have decided that the business is financially viable.** If the financial projections show that the business cannot make money, there is no need for the written portion of the plan.

The business plan should project monthly revenues and expenses for a minimum of 12 months, or if longer, until the business begins to generate positive cash flows. Why? Because new businesses incur certain expenses in the early months and it is not uncommon for start-ups to operate with a negative cash flow when the business first opens. This is typical. Long before that first sale is made, the business owner will incur numerous expenses, including attorney and accounting fees, rent deposits, store build-outs, utility deposits, signage, store fixtures, inventory, computers and software, and up-front marketing expenditures, just to name a few items.

A "negative cash flow" means that the cash expenses of the business exceed its revenues. While mentoring start-ups at SCORE, it was not uncommon for a business owner who had not prepared a business plan to say, "I want to go to my local banker and ask for a loan. I don't know how much money I should ask for. How much money do you think I need to start my business?" Without a business plan, there was no way to accurately respond to that question. On the other hand, the answer is quite simple when the financial projection portion of the business plan is completed, as that amount is easily identifiable in the business plan. That's right. **Your business plan will help you identify the amount of money needed to fund a new business venture**.

The importance of understanding the business's cash flows reminds us of two brothers we were advising who were ready to purchase a package/shipping business in January. We are sharing this story with you because it illustrates why it is so important for new business owners to conduct due diligence and work with trusted advisors. The brothers opened the meeting by informing us that they had done their homework—they merely wanted us to look for any obvious oversights they may had made. One brother planned to immediately resign from his place of employment and work full-time in the acquired business. After the business had grown substantially, the second brother would quit his job and join his sibling at work in the business. When we asked if a cash flow analysis had been done, the brothers proudly showed us the projected annual cash flows for the next five years. The analysis showed that the business generated sufficient cash flows to cover all expenses, plus a reasonable profit for the new owners. The business had strong cash flows, so they wouldn't need to invest any of their monies in the business to start. They thought it was important to proceed immediately with an offer so they would not lose this opportunity as the business broker had shared with them that several buyers were interested. I recall that when we looked at the annual cash flow numbers, they were quite impressive. If the numbers were correct, this would be an attractive investment. But then we asked a simple question. "We see that you performed an annual cash flow analysis. Did you perform a monthly cash flow analysis?" We observed that the brothers were smirking. "What's the point?" they asked us. The brothers were of the opinion that dividing the annual revenues and expenses by 12 would not change their cash flow analysis. We explained that they were correct if the exercise was to merely divide annual numbers by 12. However, we explained to them that it was important to consider seasonality's effects on the cash flows, and we further explained that certain revenues and expenses are not incurred equally each month. Rather than dividing the annual numbers by 12, the true task of a business plan is to show the actual monthly revenues and expenses for the prior and current calendar years.

About a week later we received a grateful call from the brothers. Apparently, they said, the seller had misled them. After completing a monthly cash flow analysis, the brothers learned that the business operated in the red from January through Thanksgiving. "Operating in the red" means that a business is figuratively bleeding as its cash outflows exceed its cash inflows. This packaging business generated almost all of its revenues between the Thanksgiving and Christmas holidays. This meant that the buyers needed to use their own funds to carry the business through the first 11 months because the off-season cash flows were not sufficient to pay the rent, telephone, utilities, wages, etc. They quickly realized that they had been looking at the business wearing rose-colored glasses—they never had anticipated paying these costs from personal funds. The business had now changed from one that required no capital investment from them to one that required a significant amount of their own funds to be used to run the business.

In fact, the seller had not misled these brothers, but rather they had misled themselves by not conducting a due diligence study of the business that they intended to buy. The brothers now recognized the value of working with an experience accountant and asked to meet with us again. After reviewing the purchase agreement, the franchise agreement, and the lease, we provided them with a laundry list of items to consider. First was the fact that the existing lease was going to expire within the next six months. Was the landlord willing to renew the lease? And if so, what would be the monthly rate? Their business cash flow analysis had assumed no rent increase for the first 12 months and a small cost of living increase each year thereafter. Rather than use an arbitrary rate of inflation to compute the rent expense, why not use actual figures, which were readily available from the landlord?

After the brothers asked the (seller's) business broker for more information, they were amazed to find that he refused to provide any substantiation. The broker responded by saying there were several other interested buyers who did not demand any of this information.

The brothers were told that they were at the top of the list, but they had to immediately submit an offer or walk away. The brothers asked us if we thought the broker was bluffing about other buyers being interested. Although we had no way of knowing if the broker was bluffing, we reminded them that until a couple of weeks ago, they were ready to purchase this business. It was true; there could be other buyers who would buy the business without doing sufficient due diligence. We asked the brothers a simple question: "Are you prepared to purchase this business today without knowing the answers to the critical questions you asked that the broker refused to answer?" In this case, our clients decided to walk away from the deal—not only because of the lack of information available to them to complete their due diligence, but also because they lacked the financial resources to fund the business operations for the first 11 months of the calendar year. It wouldn't have worked, since one brother would be resigning from his job to run the business and be supported by his sibling.

The cash flow projection of a business plan starts with the revenues of the business then subtracts the expenses of the business. If the revenues exceed the expenses, the business has a positive cash flow. If the expenses exceed the revenues, the business has a negative cash flow. As mentioned earlier, it is typical for many businesses to have a negative cash flow when operations are first beginning. We mention this so that the prospective business owner does not unrealistically expect his new business to generate positive cash flows from day one. You should not be discouraged to learn that the fledging business may have a period of negative cash flows.

The typical financial business plan starts with what is referred to equivalently as the income statement, the statement of profits and losses (P&L), or a statement of revenues and expenses. At the top of the P&L statement are shown the sources of revenue, and then below that, the expenses of the business. The difference between the revenues and expenses is the net profit or loss (P&L) of the company. Since we read from the top of a page to the bottom, most prospective business owners would naturally begin preparing the business plan by starting at the top of the page and projecting revenues.

Projecting revenues, in our opinion, is the most difficult part of the financial portion of the business plan, which is why we recommend beginning by identifying the expenses that the business will incur. You can ignore (for the time being) identifying revenues.

The expenses portion of your business plan is the easiest part of the financial projections. Begin by listing what we call your business' "start-up costs." These are all the expenses related to the start of the business that will likely never be incurred again. They could include attorney fees to create a legal entity, payments for licenses and certifications, rent or utility deposits, and leasehold improvements or build-outs. A build-out is when you lease space that does not meet your needs and a contractor is needed to convert the rented space. If you as the business owner will be paying for this cost, these are your build-out expenses. If the landlord agrees to pay for these, the landlord generally recoups his investment by increasing the monthly rent you pay.

If the business needs inventory or equipment (machinery, computers, furniture), identify that cost. Since these types of items (especially inventory) will need to be periodically re-purchased, consider when will those replacements occur? Then recurring expenses need to be identified. Monthly recurring items (such as rent) can be inserted in the projection. There may be certain expenses that will be incurred on fixed dates during the year, such as liability and fire insurance. These types of expenses might be paid annually, semi-annually, or in some cases monthly. Your trusted insurance agent will provide you with your payment options and cost projections. There will also be varying monthly expenses that need to be estimated, including telephone, utilities, and seasonal labor.

When you are dollarizing your projected expenses, it is acceptable to identify a range of possible costs. For example, the cost of materials for your business has increased in the past five years between 3% and 5%. What figure should you use in your business plan? If you use the 5% figure, your cash outflows would be lower than if you used the 3% rate. It is important to remember that one of the objectives of the business plan is to help you analyze whether your business will be a financial success. If you always use the lower range when projecting your expenses, you may be foolishly setting yourself up for some financial challenges.

Talk to your accountant about what figure should be used. Perhaps using the average of 4% would be a reasonable approach. Experiment! If your business is financially successful using the more conservative 5% rate, then use that one. If the future costs increase less than 5%, your actual results will be better than your projected results—and this is always a good thing.

Once all of the expenses have been identified, estimated, and entered into the financial projections, you can now begin to work on the revenue projections. **Let us give you a valuable tip before you begin**: You now know your total expenses, so you can use those as a lever to determine what your revenues must be if the business is going to succeed.

Let's assume that your total monthly expenses total $100,000. In addition, you probably have some idea as to how much money you want to earn for yourself with the business. Let's assume you want to make $60,000 a year, which is $5,000 a month. Thus, to cover your monthly expenses and reach your target take-home pay, the business needs to generate $105,000 every month.

In addition, you likely have some idea what you will charge for your product or service. If your average selling price is $5.00, you will need to make 21,000 sales per month. If your average selling price is $1,000, then you need 105 sales per month. You get the idea—you need to ask yourself if the number of sales needed each and every month is realistic. If not, then perhaps you should consider a different business. These numbers are where the rubber meets the road when it comes to planning your business. If your expenses and revenue projections do stand up to this analysis, then you can continue with your business plan.

Let's proceed assuming that you have a large enough market to keep your customers coming, and that your business plan will allow you to make enough sales each month. Assuming all that, let's discuss the next steps you need to take in creating your business plan.

This is where your due diligence as a potential business owner will be of immense value. Rather than just taking a guess at how many customers will walk into the store, how many of those walk-ins will actually make a purchase, and what the average purchase price will be, you will use your research to fill in the blanks. This includes information you may have obtained from such sources as trade association members, cooperating out-of-state non-competitors, your observations of local competitors, and various other research resources. Rather than guessing at revenue numbers, you're using hard numbers obtained from research that can be documented. Keep in mind that if you plan on asking for a business loan from a lender, this lender will want to know how you arrived at your numbers. Take a moment and think back to that entrepreneur who showed monthly revenues of $2 million to his bank lender—at this point it becomes clear why he would have had no credibility. Without a well-executed business plan, you will not have credibility either. If you plan to meet with lenders for your business, you need to be ready to discuss how you arrived at your projections, and you must have the research to support your conclusions.

Once the revenues are entered, the business owner can now see projected monthly cash flows. As we mentioned earlier, it's not uncommon for a new business to have negative cash flows in the early months. We like to see business plans that show the accumulated monthly cash flows in addition to the monthly cash flow. For example, if the business plan for the first three months of the year shows a negative cash flow of $20,000 (remember those start-up costs) in Month One, a negative cash flow of $8,000 in Month Two, and a negative cash flow of $6,000 in Month Three, the accumulated cash flows for Month One would be $20,000; Month Two would show $28,000; and Month Three would show $34,000. Let's assume that for the first 11 months of the year the accumulated cash flows were a negative $75,000 and in Month 12 the business began generating a positive cash flow. **What has this business plan shown you? It has shown you that you need $75,000 of available capital to kick-start your business.** If you are investing $15,000 of your own money in the business, **the business plan is telling you how much money you need to borrow from a bank**. In this example, that amount would be $60,000.

We stated earlier that your business plan should be flexible; as you go forward, it will probably be revised. Use spreadsheet software such as Excel for this type of analysis. If we consider our example above, we'll need to revise our cash flow after we figure a $60,000 bank loan. Why? Because the bank wants you to repay the loan! You now need to enter the monthly payment to the bank as one of your expenditures. Naturally this will change your cash needs, as your original analysis excluded this monthly debt payment. This in turn may even change the amount you need to borrow from the bank. It's an iterative process, you see. By now you should begin to appreciate why a properly built spreadsheet for your business plan is so important.

Is the financial business plan completed? Having a business that generates positive cash flows is only part of the challenge. At this point, the entrepreneur needs to ask himself a very important question. Does he have the financial means to pay his personal household expenses, such as rent or mortgage payments, food, health care, personal utilities, etc. from his personal assets, or does he expect to use monies withdrawn from his business to pay for these expenses? Notice that we did not say, "Does he expect to have his business pay for his personal expenses?" Instead we asked "Does he expect to withdraw funds from the business to pay his personal expenses?" Is the $5,000 monthly allowance discussed above sufficient to pay his personal expenses?

For reasons discussed later in this book, a business should **NEVER** pay personal expenses from the business. If monies are needed to pay for the owner's personal expenses, they should be shown as withdrawals by the owner from the business. If the intent is to take withdrawals from the business for the owner to pay personal expenses, hopefully you see that the business plan needs to be revised to reflect these withdrawals as they will decrease available cash resources. We may now have an additional expenditure that wasn't included in our original business plan.

A word of caution is needed. There is an old accounting expression: "While figures do not lie, liars do figure." What is meant by this expression? Basically, you must be honest with yourself; if the numbers are showing negative cash flows, you cannot simply adjust them until they're positive. You must base your cash flow projection on the research data you have accumulated. If your projected cash flows are negative for an extended period of time, requiring an influx of capital beyond your financial means (the figures do not lie), you do not want to simply increase the projected sales volume by 10% or increase the selling price of your product or service to create a positive cash flow (liars do figure). The only person you are fooling by taking this approach is yourself.

Remember that the business plan is your blueprint. If an engineer building a bridge performs stress tests showing that the bridge can safely carry 2,000 vehicles at one time, but the contract calls for the bridge to have a capacity of 2,200 vehicles, the engineer cannot just alter his stress test numbers by 10% to squeeze by. Arbitrarily changing numbers to show a positive result only hides the eventual disaster.

Accountants use the terms FIFO (first in, first out) and LIFO (last in, first out) when discussing methods of accounting for inventory. Don't adopt the GIGO method of accounting: "garbage in, garbage out." Keep in mind that the business plan is a very effective tool if used properly. If you misuse it intentionally, you will only postpone the eventual financial disaster, and your bridge will come crashing down just like the engineer who "massaged" his figures to support the result he wanted.

We also recommend to new business owners, who tend to be overly optimistic about the financial success of their business, that a second cash flow financial projection be completed on a "worst-case scenario basis." We believe that this is a very important step. Regardless of how thorough your due diligence, no matter how many hours you spend doing research, it's always the case that **unexpected events will occur beyond the control of the business owner**. We have seen several business owners begin paying their lease and other monthly payments just before discovering they must delay the opening of their business because of an inspection or zoning issue; difficulty obtaining licensing or permits; a contractor failing to complete his work by the promised date; or some other item that is dependent upon a third-party approval. Often this approval can come only from a township committee that meets once a month, and the process can take a few months before the approval is granted. If you experience a frustrating and unexpected event like one of these, will your business be able to survive?

We would rather see a client prepare for these unexpected events and have sufficient capital to meet them, than watch as his business fails for lack of capital. This is the beauty of using an Excel worksheet to project your cash flows. Once you've developed your base case, it is quite easy to change an assumption or two to generate the "worst case" scenario. Because the cash flow analysis tracks the business's projected cash flows and tells the business owner how much capital will be needed to fund the business operations, the owner will immediately know how much capital he must borrow to cover those unexpected events. When we discuss funding the business in Chapter 9, we recommend that the business be funded using the "worst-case" scenario rather than a best case or expected scenario. When it comes to start-up capital, you'll always be better off having too much than not enough. Banks will readily accept pre-payments of debt. On the other hand, if your business is experiencing financial difficulties and you ask for an additional loan, your loan officer will have to question whether giving you the loan will help salvage the original loan or if the bank will be throwing money out the window?

The cash flow projection worksheet is also used to evaluate other financial considerations. It can be used to identify the business's gross profit margin, net profit margin, comparison to industry ratios, and break-even analysis (the volume of sales needed to cover the cost of sales, operating expenses, and loan repayments). The cash flow projection also provides you and any other person (such as a lender) a means to compare how your business is doing compared to industry standards. If you are showing a gross profit margin of 55% and the industry standard is 40%, or if you plan to grow annual revenues at the rate of 15% and the industry standard is 10%, you must be able to explain those differences, or the credibility of your financial projection will be lost.

A very important part of the business plan is a detailed explanation of your assumptions.

If you show revenues growing at 15%, you need to document the resources you used to arrive at that growth rate. If several sources show the same growth rate, document all of those resources. Often, rather than finding several sources that show the same growth percentage, you will find varying revenue growth percentages. In such cases, you likely should take a conservative approach. Perhaps you ignore the highest and lowest growth percentages and then take an average of the remaining growth percentages you found in your research. Keep in mind that other people will be reviewing your business plan. They will want to know how you arrived at your assumptions; they'll compare your assumptions to those known to them. The appendix of your business plan should contain the sources for your assumptions and how you arrived at your figures. Check with your accountant to make sure your percentage growth rate fits with expectations.

In summary, if the business plan's financial projection shows that the business needs capital of $500,000 and your financial resources are limited to $100,000, you know that you need $400,000 of financing. Again, if the worst-case scenario shows that you will need $600,000, you should seek $500,000 of financing to avoid a shortage of needed capital to keep your business afloat.

Now that you know how much capital you need for your business, where do you find that money?

CHAPTER 9

How to Finance Your Business?

The two most common ways to finance your business are either with debt or with equity capital. For the purposes of this chapter, we are primarily focusing on funds needed to start your business. Portions of this chapter are also applicable to those who wish to expand their existing business. We briefly mention equipment loans, which are typically given to existing businesses to purchase or replace equipment. In certain situations where a new business is seeking a loan from a lender that includes the acquisition of machinery or equipment, the lender may desire to execute a separate loan agreement for such equipment purchases, using the equipment as partial collateral for the loan. There are other methods for business financing. Accounts receivables factoring, where the business uses its accounts receivable to obtain financing, is primarily a funding alternative for existing businesses that have strong accounts receivables and need a short-term infusion of capital.

Debt capital is the term that describes funding your business using borrowed money, whether these funds are advances to the business from the business owner or monies borrowed from family, friends, credit unions, banks or other lenders. For purposes of simplicity, in this book we will group commercial lenders along with traditional banks or lenders.

When you get a small business loan, you receive cash from the lender, and as the borrower, you *promise to pay back* the borrowed funds over a stated period of time, plus interest. The terms of each loan may vary, but the usual components of a loan include the amount of the debt (the money borrowed), loan period (the time span over which the loan will be repaid (e.g., 5, 15, 25 years), often expressed in terms of months, the interest rate expressed in percentage terms (such as 4 percent; either fixed or variable), and the frequency of the periodic payments that the borrower must remit to the lender (e.g., monthly, quarterly, or annual). This information is then used to compute the actual amount of the periodic loan payment.

The lender will want to see a detailed breakdown showing the amount of funds needed for each business purpose. Rather than a borrower simply asking for $150,000 for his business, the lender would prefer to see specific amounts: $20,000 for the franchise fee, $15,000 to purchase machinery and equipment, $10,000 for inventory, and the balance to sustain the company's working capital for the first year or so until it generates positive cash flows. The bank has different lending approval levels and may find it more desirable to grant a single business more than one loan. This may also require that different bank departments approve the loan requests. Whereas the borrower may be looking for a 10-year term, the bank may wish to lend the $15,000 for the business equipment over a 5-year term, as this may better represent the life of those assets serving as collateral.

There are numerous factors that a lender will consider before lending money to a business. These factors include the business purpose of the loan, length of time the business has been in existence, the strength of historic performance, and acceptability of the collateral securing the loan. These factors are discussed in more detail later in this chapter. As you read about these factors, hopefully you will see that lending to a new business rather than an existing business (with its historical track record) means greater risk to the lender. *This lack of historical performance means you, as the hopeful new business owner, must have a very strong business plan.* Likewise, if an existing business hopes to expand operations into a new market or to add a new line of business, it would also benefit from having a business plan.

Twenty years ago, the source of funding for the small business owner was to visit the local bank and speak to a loan officer with whom the business owner had a long relationship. The business owner kept an account with the local bank and was frequently seen by the banking officers (who also made a career at that bank) forming a customer relationship over the years. When the business owner asked the bank for a loan for his own business, that personal relationship and trust was often the key criteria as to whether the loan was granted. Before 2008, banks were often more than willing to give out loans to customers whose credit was not very good. But that was then—today, times have changed, as evidenced by large national banks that are now more prominent than small local banks. In addition, bank personnel are constantly moving between branches, making it more difficult to form a personal relationship with your banker.

Today when you go to a bank for a loan, you likely do not know personally the lending officer, and perhaps more importantly, the lending officer likely does not know you. Years ago, you had to go to the bank to make a deposit or withdrawal. You had to interact with the bank's employees on at least a weekly basis. Today, you can make deposits using the after-hours bank deposit drop box; you can deposit checks using a check scanner; you can use ACH debit or e-check deposits; use an Internet bank; make your bank transactions online rather than at the bank; and make withdrawals from an ATM machine after normal banking hours. All of these do not require that you meet your bank employees face to face at all. These changes in how we do banking today impair the development of personal relationships with the employees of the bank.

When you visit a bank and request a loan for your new business, the lender will request to see your business plan. This is the first stumbling block for many people who want to start a business—often they do not have a business plan. In such cases, the bank loan officer will recommend that the business owner return with a business plan. In Chester County, Pennsylvania, many of the bankers also recommend that the entrepreneur make an appointment with SCORE. Naturally you will have already completed this step. In addition, if you've completed your due diligence and formed your business plan, you will have cash flow projections and the amount of money you will need to borrow. In short, you'll be all ready to sit down with the loan officer.

It is important that borrowers realize how a business loan is underwritten. Although each lender has its own requirements, the steps to underwrite a business loan are fairly consistent among all lenders. *The lender is in the business of making a loan to make a profit.* Since bad loans negatively impact the lender's financial results, the lender wants to minimize any risk of loss associated with non-payment by the borrower. How does the bank reduce its risk? Of course, the bank reduces risk by performing due diligence on the borrower and the business. We had previously discussed the importance of due diligence when writing a business plan. The banker will also perform due diligence, reviewing and analyzing the assumptions and projections in the business plan to see how realistic they are.

The Five Cs. Lenders often refer to their due diligence as the Five Cs. While each bank may have a slightly different name for each category, the underlying concepts are the same. Let's take a peek at what is meant by the Five Cs.

The Character of the borrower is principally determined by the borrowers' FICO score. The FICO score is a means of measuring risk by looking at a person's credit history. Scores range from a low of 300 to a high of 850. Lenders will request a credit history and FICO score from one or more of the three major credit bureaus. If more than one score is obtained from different credit bureaus, the lender will often take an average of the FICO scores. The lender uses the credit report to learn more about the integrity of the borrower. The credit report will show the history of loans and whether the loan payments were made on time or late, and if the loans were repaid. This report will also identify the current debt of the borrower, the period of time of credit history (the longer the period, the higher the score), and the amount of recent credit the borrower has requested.

Cash flow (or capacity) is a determination of whether the business has the ability to generate sufficient cash flows to service the debt. For an established business, the lender will likely request a cash flow statement (formerly called a statement of sources and application of funds). If the borrower's financial statements do not include a cash flow statement, the lender will compute the cash flows from the business's other financial statements.

Lenders like to independently verify the financial information received from borrowers. For existing businesses, this confirmation process includes requesting copies of the three most recent years' of income tax returns (business and personal) and the execution of IRS Form 4506-T. The tax returns will be used by the lender to verify the accuracy of the financial information submitted by the borrower. The lender uses Form 4506-T to obtain direct confirmation with the IRS that the tax returns you have provided match the returns filed with the IRS. The lender also wants to make sure that the business owner is filing his tax returns. If the business owner is not paying his income taxes to the IRS, the IRS could be in the process of placing a lien on the very assets that the bank is considering using as collateral.

Since a start-up business has no historical records to evaluate, there will be a greater emphasis placed on the borrower's personal credit and personal financial statement. The lender will definitely want to review the personal tax returns for the past three years. In addition, the lender will carefully scrutinize the business plan's cash flow projections. The lender will not only focus on the cash flows as reflected on the business plan, but also scrutinize the assumptions used in the business plan. In other words, lenders will carefully "scrub the numbers" for reasonableness.

Using this financial information, the lender will compute the borrower's **debt service coverage ratio** (DSCR). The DSCR is the ratio of cash available to service the debt relative to the principal and interest payments on that debt. The numerator (cash available) is equal to the borrower's net income plus non-cash expenditures (examples would be depreciation and amortization) plus the add-back of interest expense less distributions and withdrawals made by the business owner. The denominator of the ratio is the sum of the current debt service (principal and interest) payments.

If the DSCR ratio is less than 1.0, it indicates that the borrower has negative cash flows and is a poor credit risk. Many lenders require a DSCR of 1.2. This ratio indicates that the borrower has positive cash flows 20% greater than the amount needed to service his debt. Naturally, once you understand how the ratio is used, it is easy to understand that the higher the ratio, the easier it is to obtain a loan. The higher ratios provide comfort to the lender in that if the business's actual results are not as good as those projected in the business plan, that the business owner will still be able to make his debt service payments. While the DSCR computation is often done for the business alone, the lender may also include the owner's personal cash flow analysis (a global approach).

In Appendix B, we have included an example to show how to compute the DSCR ratio.

Collateral is viewed by the lender as a secondary source of repayment should the borrower be unable to repay the loan. During the loan process, fledging small business owners are often surprised to find that lenders want collateral as part of the loan agreement. Small business owners are often under the impression that the bank merely loans funds to business owners who ask for the money. While that practice may have been true some years ago, it is no longer a common approach today.

Lenders look at the company's balance sheet to identify assets that are available to repay debt. Existing businesses should have a balance sheet or what is sometimes referred to as a statement of assets, liabilities, and equity. The new business owner should work with his CPA to create a beginning balance sheet from the business plan. The lender will also very likely review the personal financial statement of the borrower to identify assets to repay or support the payment of the debt. A personal financial statement is a listing of the fair market value of the personal assets owned by the borrower less the liabilities or debts or the borrower. The difference between the assets and liabilities is the net worth of the borrower. The lender will also look at the type of assets owned and the liquidity of those assets. If a loan goes bad and the bank is forced to recover assets, a certificate of deposit at the lending institution will be a more liquid and attractive option than foreclosing on real estate.

If your business will be co-owned by your partner in marriage, the lender will usually want both spouses to be co-signers. If you are both owners of the business or are employed by the business, the lender will usually request that both spouses sign the loan agreement. If the credit of one business owner is not very good, or if the DSCR is not within the bank's lending policies, the lending officer may look for other means to secure the loan. In such cases, and where the spouse is not a co-owner or employee, the banker may be precluded by federal regulation from requiring (or asking) that the spouse co-sign the loan. In such cases, the lender may deny the loan, or look for a specifically defined credit reason to request the spouse's signature. The authors are not attorneys and cannot render legal advice; thus it is best that you consult an attorney regarding your lender's requirements or questions.

Capital is the net worth of the business. A lender may define net worth as the sum of the capital invested by the business owner in his business plus the cumulative earnings (or losses) of the business. The cumulative earnings are often referred to as the retained earnings of the business by accountants.

One of the most popular financial ratios is the **debt-to-equity** leverage ratio. A lender will compute this ratio as an indicator of the business's financial health. It is computed by dividing the company's total debt (short-term and long-term) by the company's equity (debt plus capital contributed by the owner). Debt must be repaid over a period of time. But if that capital is invested into a business as equity, it may not be required to be repaid in the event of bankruptcy. Assuming everything else is equal, this should explain why the higher the debt-to-equity ratio, the riskier the loan to the lender.

The bank will also review the **interest coverage** ratio. This ratio measures the business's ability to meet its interest obligations using the income earned by the business. It is computed by dividing net operating income by interest expense. If the ratio is close to one or less than one, it is indicative that the business may have difficulties in paying its interest.

Net worth is often considered to be an irrelevant accounting term— it has little correlation to the fair market value of a business. For an existing business, the lender may require that a valuation study be done by a certified appraiser to determine the fair market value of the business. When a valuation study is done, a certified appraiser looks at the historical cash flows of the business (along with other factors) to determine an approximate value for the business. But this valuation is very flexible, particularly when it comes to the value of the "goodwill" of the business. "Goodwill" and "going concern" are terms that are sometimes used interchangeably. These are intangible assets that you cannot see or touch. An existing business has certain attributes that a new business does not have. Examples would include an existing customer base, a reputation in the community for the quality of its product (or service), and its customer service relationships, because some customers have more confidence when dealing with an established business than with a start-up. Because of the nature of these intangible assets, they are more challenging assets to value for an existing business.

Because a start-up business lacks historical performance, the valuation of the business is a more subjective test. If the new business has inventory and machinery and equipment, the lender may use a liquidation value for these assets. However, since the new business lacks a customer base and reputation, the lender will likely view it as having no goodwill or going concern value.

Lenders also like to see if the business owner is accruing cash in the business or immediately withdrawing the cash from the business. An owner who does not leave the cash in the business may be viewed negatively by the lender as an owner who is not committed to growing the business or as someone who may lack confidence in the business.

Conditions includes a review of the industry and its inherit risks. Some lenders will not make loans to start-up companies or certain industries based on their experience in that industry, the net profit margins for that industry, or because of legal concerns about the increased environmental and liability hazards of certain industries. Other lenders may loan to a business in an industry that it has concerns about, but may require a DSCR of greater than 1.2X.

Before making a loan application at a bank, it is worth your efforts to inquire if the bank is willing to make a loan to a start-up business or one in your industry. The local SBA office may be a good source to identify a lender willing to lend to your industry or that is willing to loan to a start-up business.

A lender will also consider the overall state of the economy—is it growing or shrinking? How aggressive is the competition in your industry? Is the industry in a state of growth or is it declining? The lender will compare your risk factors and ratios against other borrowers in its portfolio. In addition, the lender has an unlimited source to learn more about your industry and its strengths, weaknesses and trends—the Internet.

The reader may find the book titled "Small–Business Loan Request Guide," written by Ted Nichols, to be a valuable resource. The guide summarizes how the small-business owner can prepare for a bank loan application. Mr. Nichols had a 42-year career in the banking industry working primarily in small business lending. You can obtain a copy of this guide by contacting XLibris Corporation at 1-888-795-4274 or orders@xlibris.com.

Loans from the U.S. Small Business Association

As part of the federal government, the SBA has a mission to promote small business growth in the USA. Its employees are dedicated to helping Americans start and grow a business, and because jobs are created when small businesses expand, the result is good for the USA. The SBA accomplishes its mission with its "3Cs and a D" program:

- Counseling small business owners (this is where SCORE mentoring fits)
- Capital provision in the form of business loans
- Contracting
- Disaster Assistance

Since this chapter is focusing on sources of capital to finance a business, we are not addressing the SBA's programs for Contracting and Disaster Assistance. The SBA's counseling program for small business owners (SCORE) is addressed elsewhere in this book.

Focusing on Capital, one of the ways that the SBA promotes small business is by delivering millions of loans and loan guarantees to small businesses. Since the SBA has a variety of loan programs that are dependent upon the dollar amount size of the loan and how the proceeds will be used; there are also special loan promotions such as loans for women and minority business owners. Some loans available through the SBA place special requirements on lenders. Because of the vast array of possible loans, the business owner should get familiar with the SBA's programs to find one that suits the needs of the business. You can learn much more about the SBA loan programs and find the contact information for your local SBA lenders by ZIP code on the www.sba.gov website.

The SBA does not offer grants, and the agency does not directly lend funds to the business. Instead, the SBA acts as an intermediary between banks and entrepreneurs, guaranteeing a portion of the loan made by the lender to the business. The SBA guarantee is a fallback for lenders that wish to make loans, but who need some further assurance they will be paid back. This guarantee helps entrepreneurs secure loans even when they may represent a greater risk of default than the lender would normally consider.

How small must your business be to obtain an SBA loan? The SBA's definition of a small business is based on two principal factors: number of employees and gross revenues. The SBA also requires that the business have control of its business cash flows and profits. If you are a franchisee where the franchisor has the right to withdraw funds from your business account unilaterally (excluding certain expenses such as royalties), your business may not qualify for an SBA loan. The SBA also does not lend to non-profit organizations. Having said that, the SBA's criteria are very broad, and we understand that about 95% of American businesses meet the definition of a small business for the purposes of the SBA. In fact, in the United States, there are over 28 million small businesses individually owned by three or fewer owners.

By understanding some of the basics of SBA loans, you will be able to better position yourself both to secure financing and to obtain more favorable loan terms. *These loan terms are very important to your business, as they will determine your monthly payments (cash out the door).* As a business owner, one of your primary objectives is to effectively manage your cash flows—many a viable business has been ruined because of insufficient cash flow to meet operating costs as it awaits payment for its goods or services. If you can negotiate a better interest rate and amortization period for your loan, you will improve your company's cash flows by decreasing the outflow of cash to service debt, and in the process, improve your chances of success.

Please refer to Appendix C to learn about the different types of SBA loans, why some lenders prefer SBA loans, how SBA loan terms may vary from lender to lender, and the perceived advantage of working with a lender who has been designated as a Preferred Lending Partner by the SBA.

Home equity loans

Assuming that there is equity in your personal residence, a home equity loan may be the most cost effective way to borrow money for a start-up. A home's equity is the difference between the fair market value of the home less any debt on the residence. In other words, if you sold your home and paid off your home loan, how much cash (equity) would you have left over? These loans are sometimes viewed as dangerous by the small-business owner, because if the business fails then the bank would foreclose on the owner's personal residence. It is important to note that one of the C's discussed earlier was Collateral. If the borrower has a personal residence, the lender will likely demand to place a lien on that home to securitize the loan before it is originated. Thus, using a home equity loan or home equity line of credit (HELOC) may be no riskier than a bank loan, since both types of loans require the personal residence as collateral. A home equity loan may have more favorable terms of interest and payback period than many business loans. Many HELOC loans do not require a monthly payment, which will give you greater flexibility in managing your monthly debt service payments.

Personal loans

A personal loan occurs when the business owner, family members, or friends pay money into the business with the expectation of repayment. In our experience, this has been the most prevalent type of loan for start-up businesses. In our tax practice, one of the questions we often are asked is: "I made a personal loan to my business or to a relative or friend, and it went bad. Can I now write that off as a tax expense?" Although this book's focus is to help the business owner to be successful, we do realize that some businesses fail. In this case, the tax implications vary; some people are able to successfully write off bad debt, but it will depend upon your situation and whether the loan was originated for personal or business use as defined by the Internal Revenue Service. We have included some guidelines in Appendix D; however, tax laws are constantly changing and each situation is determined by the facts and circumstances. These guidelines are not to be construed as tax advice.

You must always consult with an experienced tax professional in these cases.

Equity capital

Equity capital occurs when someone invests in your business and shares in the success (or failure) of the business. It is theoretically no different than the investor buying shares in a stock traded on the NYSE (New York Stock Exchange). If the stock appreciates in value, the investor's initial investment will increase, and he "makes" money. If the stock depreciates in value, the investor "loses" money. We used the terms "makes" and "loses" because these gains or losses are unrealized until such time that the equity owner sells the stock interest. When the owner actually sells the stock to another party, the gain or loss on this investment is realized for tax reporting purposes.

A business owner is often attracted by the thought of taking on investors in the business. The motivation is that when the owner gets a loan from a lender, the loan must be repaid and those monthly debt service payments must be made. However, when issuing stock to a new investor, the business owner receives an immediate infusion of cash, but he does not need to make any monthly payments, and does not have to repay the monies received. While taking on an equity investor (compared to a business loan) may sound like a no-brainer, there are complications. Aside from close relatives who are willing to ignore the economics and financial realities of this type of financing, it is very difficult to find such an equity investor. Why? Because of two significant differences between investing in a small business versus a business traded on a public exchange such as the New York Stock Exchange.

These two differences are "known value" and "liquidity." When one invests in a publicly traded company, it is easy to monitor unrealized gains and losses (or "paper" gains or losses) by going on the Internet or by reading a financial publication such as *The Wall Street Journal*. This is because there are always other investors buying and selling the same business, so the current market price is readily available on various public forums. On the other hand, when one makes an equity investment in a small business that is not publicly traded, the day-to-day value of that business is unknown. So if you find a willing investor, what percentage of the business should be given for the amount of his investment? Is his $25,000 investment worth 10% of the business? Maybe. But it is very hard to know. Your business *might* be worth $250,000, but on the other hand, perhaps that investor's investment is actually worth 60% of your business, which values your business at only about $42,000. For this reason and others discussed in this book, business owners should periodically have a valuation study done by a certified valuation expert. The valuation study will show the possible ranges of values for a company on a particular date.

The second major difference is the lack of liquidity. Whereas stocks traded on the NYSE are easily traded and can be converted into cash almost instantaneously, small business stock is usually not publicly traded and thus there is not a market of buyers readily available. Thus an owner of stock who wishes to sell his equity investment may not find a willing buyer. Even if a buyer is found, another factor that will likely negatively impact the value of that equity interest is the market value discount associated with having a minority interest. If the new buyer purchases 10% of the equity of the business, he is a minority owner with little or no say in how the business is run. He will face the same illiquidity issue if he wants to cash out his equity interest in the future. Thus, any savvy buyer who has consulted with a tax professional and financial advisor will never pay full value for the seller's equity. This discount reflects both the seller's minority interest and the lack of liquidity for his stock. So if the business had a valuation study that showed it is worth $250,000, a 10% minority interest would not be worth $25,000 due to the discounts that the well-advised investor will expect because of these reasons.

If the owner gives up more than 50% of the equity of the business, he will no longer retain control of his business. Thus, the owner will generally never want to relinquish control of his small business. This makes finding equity investors who would own a minority interest very difficult to find (outside of family members). In those few situations where the owner may find a minority investor, that person will want to be kept advised of all business decisions. If the minority owner does not agree with those decisions, you will undoubtedly find that you have a disgruntled co-owner, which makes for a very uncomfortable situation.

Crowdfunding

Crowdfunding is a relatively recent development in start-up funding. We think it needs to be mentioned as more and more people have found it to be a successful means to obtain financing. The Wikipedia definition of crowdfunding is a "collective effort of individuals who network and pool their money, usually via the Internet, to support efforts initiated by other people or organizations." Crowdfunding is also referred to as crowd financing, equity crowdfunding, and crowd-sourced fundraising. Crowdfunding is sometimes referred to as funding a company's financial needs by selling small amounts of equity to numerous investors. Think of crowdfunding as an individual business owner meeting his goal by receiving small contributions from many parties, the crowd of people, who support the project or venture.

There are currently two main models for crowdfunding. There is the donation-based model where persons donate money to the business in return for products, perks or rewards. The second model is often referred to as "investment crowdfunding," where businesses that need capital offer investors an interest in the company in the form of debt or equity. With this model, the lenders have the potential of a financial return beyond a simple perk or reward.

Forbes.com has printed on the Internet the "Top 10 Crowdfunding Sites for Fundraising." Our readers may find it helpful to learn more about this concept and pay a visit to those sites that have had funding success.

Seed money may be available to those businesses that have the potential to generate jobs. This money is set aside by local and state governments to aid in economic expansion. The borrower should arrange a meeting with a local state representative to learn what state or local programs are available. These kinds of financing are particularly available in the fields of science and technology because of their potential for growth.

Grants are favorably viewed by new business owners who are looking for so called "free money." Unlike business loans, grants do not have to be repaid, which is a real advantage to start-ups. However, grants are generally restricted to very specific types of businesses. If you are interested in researching grants that may be available for your business, you should contact the SBA about federal grants; and get in touch with your state and local congressional representatives about grants that may be available at different levels of government. Another useful resource for private and foundation grants is the public library, which may subscribe to grant databases with continually updated information about applying for grants.

Enterprise zones

These are specific geographical areas that have been designated by a governmental authority. If a business operates within an enterprise zone, it may be entitled to receive various types of financial aid. These aid packages can include tax benefits (e.g., reduced real estate taxes), special financing terms (e.g., lower interest rates or repayment terms), and other benefits offered as a means to encourage businesses to establish and maintain a presence within specific geographical areas. These incentives are often linked to job creation initiatives to hire local residents in an enterprise zone to stimulate economic growth.

ROBS (Rollovers as Business Start-Ups)

ROBS is the IRS acronym for Rollovers as Business Start-Ups. These opportunities are often recommended by franchisors and business brokers to people who may lack capital or financing, but who want to start their own business using retirement funds.

We were hesitant to mention this type of financing out of concern that our readers may think this is the ideal way to finance a new business or that we are promoting this type of financing. In fact, we believe ROBS opportunities are often misrepresented and can be very risky to entrepreneurs who do not consider the dangers involved with using retirement funds to start a business. We finally decided to include a ROBS discussion because we believe that there are too many promoters of this type of financing who do not properly disclose and explain the pitfalls associated. In short, we wanted our readers to better understand the hazards of using this type of financing.

If you are considering using ROBS, we recommend that you first consult with a CPA and legal counsel who are familiar with these transactions so that you thoroughly understand the details and potential pitfalls.

In our office, we have done analyses under different scenarios showing the after-tax results of using ROBS financing, and in most cases, those results showed that the business owner would have been better off using a different financing model.

For those readers who are considering ROBS or who have already financed their business using this method of financing, you will find Appendix E of immense interest.

CHAPTER 10

What Type Of Legal Entity Is Best For Your Business?

Before we get started on this chapter, we wish to reiterate that we are not attorneys, we do not render legal advice, and that you should always consult with competent legal counsel with respect to legal matters. By "competent legal counsel," we refer to an attorney who has the training and experience to help you resolve the legal issues that you will encounter in your small business.

Remember in an earlier chapter that we discussed the importance of the business owner first identifying a viable business concept and creating a business plan to show that the business will generate sufficient cash flows to be successful. These two steps are the basic building blocks to determine the feasibility of starting a business. Unfortunately, far too often when we meet with a start-up business owner for the first time, we learn that the owner has obtained his employer identification number (EIN) from the IRS and has already created the legal entity before doing any other feasibility work. The owner now wishes to consult with a CPA to ensure that he is compliant with IRS rules and regulations. We've all heard the analogy of "putting the cart in front of the horse," and this is an appropriate situation to invoke that phrase. If we ask why, we commonly hear that it was an easy step to complete. The business owner knew he needed an EIN for the business, and since it's easy to complete online using the IRS's website, he did it. You know: something to cross off the list of to-do's when starting a new business. From our perspective, when he applied for his EIN or created his company, he also may have bypassed some tax planning strategies, weakened his asset protection framework, and increased his future tax liabilities. Of course, in most cases these mistakes can be corrected, but only at an added cost. It is always less expensive to do something right the first time than to fix it the second time around. This is no different than hiring the least expensive building contractor to erect an addition to your home, only to find out later that there was no foundation laid, or that the structure wasn't built to code. The cost to remove the initial walls and pour a proper foundation is more expensive than if the job had been done correctly from the start.

In the situation described above, the business owner has leapfrogged the two steps that are vital to determining if he has a viable business, and he has disregarded the due diligence required to formulate a business plan. He may have no understanding as to how his new legal entity is taxed; but since taxes are determined by the type of legal framework chosen, these decisions will affect cash flows. If the business owner does not understand how his legal entity will be taxed, how can he properly compute the cash flows in his business plan? The simple answer is that he cannot.

Do yourself a favor—conserve your capital resources and the time you will need to spend to start your business; follow an orderly plan when you start a business as outlined by your trusted advisors.

Each state requires that a company register when doing business within that state's borders. The qualification process usually requires the business owner to file with the state's Department of State to obtain a certificate of authority to operate. The filing documents usually require the name of the company, the principal business address, the purpose of the business, and the name of a registered agent for that business within the state. Some states require that the business owners and their personal addresses be identified. Most states allow the business owner to serve as the company's registered agent if the business owner resides in that state. A registered agent is required in case the state needs to send the business an official notice. If the state mails its notice to the registered agent, that notice is deemed to have been properly served to the business. The annual cost to engage a registered agent is usually in the range of $100 to $200. We think it is best that the business hire a registered agent who does this for a living, and who is intimately familiar with the state's rules and requirements.

When registering to do business in its state of incorporation or formation, a business is considered to be a domestic business. The term "domestic" refers to that particular state, not to the entire United States. Likewise, when a company registers to do business in a state outside its state of formation, it is considered a "foreign" company, even though it is a U.S.-based business.

Creating Your Legal Entity

When considering what type of legal entity to choose, you need to consider the value of limited liability protection. Limiting your legal liability means that if you are sued and are found liable, you want to minimize which of your assets can be considered in the suit. You need to understand that not all legal entities provide the same degree of asset protection (minimizing legal liability).

We believe that the five most important aspects of limiting your liability are as follows:

- Who creates your legal entity
- Choice of legal entity
- Selecting the state where your company will be formed based on its asset protection legislation and case law history
- An LLC operating agreement or corporate bylaws written to provide the greatest amount of asset protection
- Carrying adequate insurance coverage

Who Creates Your Legal Entity

There are three fundamental ways to create a legal entity. These are:

- Use an Internet service
- Do it yourself
- Engage legal counsel

Let's take a brief look at each of these options. Regardless of which option is used, when selecting a name for your business you should consider at least two alternative names in case the name you prefer has been selected by another company and is not available to be used by you.

Internet Incorporation Services

There are business owners who engage an Internet company to form a legal entity for their start-up. Obviously, entrepreneurs who go this route are seeking to keep expenses to a minimum or are unaware of the value of using a business attorney. In truth, this method is easy—you make a phone call and within a half-hour and for $200 or less (depending upon the state) you have your legal entity created. The problem with this approach is that the business owner has merely created a legal entity that allows him to use a business name and to be qualified to do business in that state. The method does not give personalized legal advice as to whether you should be operating as a LLC, corporation, or limited liability partnership. As a new business owner, you may not have chosen the best legal structure for your industry, or you may be exposing yourself to unnecessary legal liability. The potential problems may include the choice of state where the legal entity was created or an operating agreement or by-laws that do not contain the proper asset protection language. Of course, the legal entity that you choose can also cause you to pay more in income and payroll taxes than you need to.

Do It Yourself

The business owner may be able to create a company in a state by filing the proper documents and paying the filing fees; details of which are usually found on the Department of State's website. It is likely that this approach is slightly less expensive than using an Internet service provider, but do you really want to play the role of attorney for your business with so much at stake? In short, you assume the same asset protection risks as if you had used an Internet incorporation service.

Engage Legal Counsel

We've all heard the adage: "You get what you pay for." It is our opinion that if a business owner is investing a considerable amount of money in a new business venture, if he is in a business that needs asset protection, or if he's going into business with a partner, it is imperative to engage competent legal counsel. Again, we do not wish to offend any attorneys. We, the authors, are not implying that some attorneys are incompetent; rather, we believe that the business owner must take the time to find and engage an attorney who is <u>experienced in business law</u>. The cost for an attorney to create a legal entity would likely be in the range of $1,000 to $3,000 depending on various factors.

The business owner may be tempted to ask a family member or a close friend who is an attorney to create the business entity and draft the necessary legal documents. Please be careful with this approach as well. When business owners use friends and relatives who are attorneys to create their legal entity, and those attorneys do not have experience creating legal entities, we believe there is a great disservice being done. If you or a member of your family were to experience chest pains, would you rush to see a dermatologist or a proctologist because they were cheaper than a heart specialist? Of course not—you would never think twice about it; you would consult with a qualified and experienced physician. Nevertheless, business owners jeopardize their financial well-being every day by consulting with attorneys (and accountants) who are not specialists. If you are a business owner and you believe that one accountant, attorney, lender, or insurance agent is as good as any other, you may find to your detriment that you were mistaken. Please continue searching for an experienced professional who can bring added value to your business during all the years it will be in business.

When the business owner meets with his attorney and requests that the attorney create a legal entity, we believe that it is very important that the business owner, accountant, and insurance agent be part of that decision-making process, rather than allowing the attorney to make that decision by himself. Since it is quite easy to create a legal entity, and since the attorney is a member of the trusted team of advisors who is responsible for creating the business entity, we recommend that the other members of your team be part of this decision-making process for reasons discussed later in this chapter.

Choice of Legal Entity

There are four basic legal entities. These are:

- Sole Proprietorship
- Partnership
- Corporation
- LLC

Sole Proprietorship

There will be some entrepreneurs who decide to go into business in the most simple and inexpensive way. Rather than creating a partnership, corporation or a limited liability company (LLC), which requires registering with a state's Department of State and Department of Revenue, this person decides to be a sole proprietor. Without doubt, this is the least costly way to start a business. Why pay an attorney to create a legal company when the entrepreneur can form his own company at absolutely no cost? Furthermore, why pay a CPA to prepare a corporate or partnership business tax return when the entrepreneur can include the tax filing in his personal income tax return using Schedule C?

It is our opinion that the sole proprietor model is the second worst way to operate a business. The reason is quite simple: this form of business offers you absolutely no asset protection. From a legal liability perspective, if the business is sued, all of the sole proprietor's personal assets are at risk. Thus, while this form of ownership may be perceived as the least expensive way to form a business, it could easily be the most expensive form of ownership if you are sued and found liable. Ah, but this begs the question: "What is the *worst* form of business structure?" For those of you who are wondering, read on.

Partnership

We believe that the worst form of business ownership is a general partnership. With this type of ownership, you could wind up not only being sued for your actions, but also for the actions of your general partners. Partnerships are required to file IRS Form 1065, and each partner receives an annual form K-1 from the partnership that shows the partner's share of income and expenses that are to be reported on his personal income tax return. A partnership may require that the partners file personal income tax returns in several states if the partnership does business in those states.

To limit legal liability, businesses often use a limited partnership model, which may have one or more general partners (GP) and one or more limited partners (LP). If properly structured by legal counsel, the limited partners' legal liability is limited to their investment in the partnership. The GP is then the only party who would be personally liable. A more advanced planning technique would be to use a corporation or limited liability company (LLC) as the GP to further limit liability.

Corporation or Limited Liability Company (LLC)

When attorneys select the type of legal entity for the small business owner who is concerned with limiting legal liability, there appears to be two major schools of thought. Attorneys are split between starting the business as a corporation or as an LLC. Since corporations and LLCs both provide limited liability protection, the attorney may think that choosing between the two is not an issue. Our personal (non-legal opinion) preference is that LLCs provide the business with the best combination of legal protection and tax minimization. Our preference for the LLC legal entity is based on numerous conversations we have had with attorneys who specialize in asset protection and who recommend the use of LLCs over corporations for reasons discussed later in this chapter under the heading "Asset Protection."

We have met with new clients who contacted us after creating their legal entity to say that the attorney informed them *after* creating the legal entity that he was not a tax expert and that the client should consult with his accountant to ensure that all tax matters are properly addressed. Think about that advice. Isn't one of the most important aspects of choosing a legal entity is to reduce taxes paid? The attorney is creating the legal entity and then in effect is telling the client to meet with his accountant after the legal entity was formed to determine how to minimize taxes. These attorneys are doing a great disservice to their clients. Armed with this knowledge, the business owner needs to insist that his attorney and tax professional are working together and all parties agree upon the type of legal entity that will be formed and the reasons why.

When we meet with business owners whose attorney created a legal entity and then told them to seek advice from a tax professional, we always ask: "Why did your attorney choose this particular form of legal entity?" Usually, the business owner has no idea. He relied solely upon the attorney doing the right thing. If the business was incorporated, the owner does not know if he is a C Corporation or an S Corporation.

The attorney may have decided that the client should choose an S Corporation, but did not make finalize that tax election, thinking that the CPA would make the election. However, the CPA may not be able to make that election by the required due date because he was left out of these discussions with the attorney. There are also differences between tax entities and legal entities. For example, we've seen business owners whose attorneys created an LLC, then told the client the business "would be taxed as an LLC," without explaining that an LLC is a not a tax entity.

Pay attention to this situation. The client is about to become an entrepreneur, invest a considerable amount of his time and money to this new business venture, but he hasn't the slightest idea about what type of legal or tax entity to create and why. What a way to begin a new business! How could this have been avoided? Would it not make more sense for the client, attorney, and accountant to meet or have a telephone conference call to discuss the client's goals and needs and then form the appropriate legal entity? Of course it would.

Compare the above scenario with the following: imagine if the business owner met with his trusted team of advisors to let them know he wanted to start his own business and needed a legal entity. A discussion would ensue about the business owner's business plan and projected cash flows. Legal counsel would give his advice about the type of legal entity to best minimize legal liability; the accountant would discuss the taxability of the business cash flows and recommend the type of tax entity that would minimize income and payroll taxes; the insurance agent would address insurance coverage needs and any possible risks or exclusions for the legal entity being discussed; the banker would share what impact the legal structure of the business would have on the chances for a business loan approval. This discussion accomplished, the attorney would draft the legal documents for the appropriate legal entity. Isn't it like night and day when you consider the contributions of the two approaches toward the success of the business owner?

Selecting the State

If limited liability is of concern to the business owner, we disagree with those attorneys who automatically create the business entity in the state where its base of operations exists. An attorney may justify this move by saying that a second set of state income tax returns would need to be filed if the business is incorporated in a state outside its base of operations (which is not always correct), thus demanding additional registrations and annual fees. The attorney will say that by creating the legal entity in the state where it will be operating, the business owner will be saving on compliance and taxes.

All this may or may not be true, but it's important to consider all options if asset protection is of concern to the business owner. While there may be some additional costs to incorporating outside your state, they are not substantial; they are a "small premium" to pay each year for added legal liability protection if your attorney determines this course of action will aid your business.

It is our understanding through discussions with asset protection attorneys that the state where the business is formed is of utmost importance when considering legal liability. Since state laws differ regarding asset protection for different types of legal entities, creating a business in a state with strong pro-business asset protection legislation and case law history is a very important factor to consider.

LLC Operating Agreement or Corporate Bylaws

The operating agreement and corporate bylaws is the area where using an experienced business attorney justifies the added cost. An LLC is governed by its operating agreement, and corporations are governed by their bylaws. If you are sued by a creditor, a very well-written operating agreement (or a bylaw) that includes all of the language and provisions needed to limit the business owner's personal liability will prove to be invaluable. When you use an Internet incorporation service or if you go the route of do-it-yourself incorporation, those operating agreements will most likely contain basic provisions that do not include the specifics needed to protect you from your creditors. Remember that when you go to court, the court will be considering the merits of the creditor's case based on state law, case law precedents, and the operating agreement of the LLC (or bylaws of the corporation) to reach its decision.

Obtaining Adequate Insurance Coverage

How many times have we heard a business owner say that he is not concerned about legal liability because he is insured? We view insurance as backup asset protection not to be used as the business owner's sole or primary asset protection strategy. If all else fails, you hope that your insurance policy will cover you. Remember that all insurance policies have exclusion provisions. We have yet to meet a business owner who knew which acts were not covered by his insurance policy. Many business owners never even read their insurance policies. They asked for coverage, paid the premium, received the policy and placed the policy in a drawer not to be touched until renewal the following year. Asked how much insurance coverage he has, the business owner will affirmatively state, for example, that he's covered by a $2 million policy. But ask him what happens if a creditor is awarded twice that amount, and you may not get such a confident reply.

Asset Protection

The term "asset protection" describes the body of laws and legal techniques that can be utilized to secure you or your business from civil liability to creditors. A sound asset protection strategy attempts to shield the largest possible value of assets from creditors. Some attorneys have described a sound asset protection strategy as placing significant barriers between the creditor and the assets of their client.

When it comes to asset protection, there are two types of liabilities. An "inside liability" is a cause of action that arises from your business. For example, a lawsuit arising from a slip and fall at your place of business would be considered an inside liability. These lawsuits may affect other assets owned by your legal entity. For example, the slip and fall plaintiff is going after other assets of your business, such as your cash, accounts receivables, and other property. An "outside liability" arises from an event in your life that is not necessarily directly related to your business. Since many of you drive vehicles and have children who drive your vehicles, an automobile accident that is caused by you or your children may result in the injured plaintiff seeking to seize the ownership of your business (as well as other assets you own) to satisfy the resulting judgment.

Some industries may not be prone to liability issues. Other industries, such as bars, auto repair shops and environmental businesses will often have a much greater exposure. In addition, your business could face discrimination or harassment charges from its employees or vendors. By forming a properly structured legal entity (discussed in Chapter 11), you can better protect yourself from "inside liabilities."

If you are creating a business that has significant legal liability issues or you can't sleep at night worrying about being sued as a business owner, you should consider adding to your team of advisors an attorney who specializes in asset protection. You may be asking yourself why you need to consult with an attorney who specializes in asset protection if you already engaged a business attorney. After all, isn't the business attorney an expert in asset protection? That is an excellent question. When you conduct your due diligence to find your business attorney, ask him how many asset protection courses he took in law school and how many continuing education courses he takes each year relating to asset protection. Ask him about some of the techniques he uses to minimize legal liability and how he protects the assets of his clients. It has been our experience that the vast majority of attorneys (and accountants) have little or any practical experience in *advanced* asset protection techniques. This is not a condemnation of business law attorneys or accountants. The reason an asset protection attorney is more knowledgeable about asset protection planning strategies is that he specializes in this field. It would be unfair to expect a business attorney to have the same experience and background as an asset protection attorney. To determine if you need an asset protection attorney, a good place to start is by having a discussion of your liability concerns with your business attorney so that he can properly advise you if you need to work with legal counsel who is a specialist in asset protection.

When speaking with asset protection attorneys about "outside liabilities," they have told us that they prefer that the business operate as an LLC (or as a limited liability partnership, LLP) rather than as a corporation. They have come to this finding because in *many* states LLCs (and LLPs) receive "charging order protection." These attorneys prefer not to create a legal entity in a state that does not provide the LLC with charging order protection. These same attorneys prefer states that provide for the charging order as the sole remedy of a creditor.

According to Nolo.com,

... [I]n some states, obtaining a charging order is a creditor's exclusive remedy. These states are the most 'debtor friendly'; they provide the greatest protection for LLC owners against personal creditors. This protection extends to both the debtor/LLC member and any co-owners who would otherwise be at risk of having creditors take more aggressive action against the LLC, including possibly forcing dissolution of their LLC.

You are likely asking yourself, "What is a charging order, and why is it important?" In short, a charging order is a court order that directs the partnership or LLC to pay to the creditor any payments that it would have made to the debtor, who is also a partner or LLC member.

When working with our clients, we often find it helpful to explain certain difficult to understand issues in terms that relate to them. In this case, think of a charging order in terms of a lien on your personal residence versus a creditor foreclosing on your home. If a creditor forecloses on your home, he now owns it and can force you to move out; he can then use the home as a rental or sell it. The creditor has full control of your residence and can do as he pleases. However, if a creditor places a lien against your home, he has no say on what you do with your home. However if you try to sell, refinance, or take equity (money) out of the property, the creditor would receive any funds he was owed until the debt is satisfied or the equity is gone.

In a business setting, the charging order is comparable to the example of a lien on your home. In a state that provides charging order protection, the creditor has no voting or management rights in the operation of your business, cannot force you to make (cash or other property) distributions, and is only entitled to the money that is actually distributed from the business. If the member(s) of the LLC do not agree to make a distribution, the creditor receives nothing. This is definitely a better asset protection scenario than operating a business without charging order protection where the creditor can sell off the business assets or the entire business and distribute the cash or other property of the business to him. While at this point the concept of charging order protection may not be entirely clear, the important takeaways are that it is something that LLCs offer that corporations do not, it is of immense value to an LLC and its owners, that the protection afforded to the LLC varies by state and thus legal counsel representation is very important.

It is worth noting that when discussing charging order protection with your attorney, you should be advised that the protection might vary depending upon whether your LLC is a single-member LLC (owned by one person) or a multi-member LLC (owned by two or more persons). The purpose of charging order protection is viewed by some as a means to protect the other partners/members from judgments of the debtor. Since a single member LLC only has one owner, some courts have taken the position that the single member LLC limited liability protection can be ignored, as no other member is affected. Thus we believe that charging order protection should be a major consideration when choosing the state in which to form your LLC. In summary, these are just some of the many reasons why we believe it is so important that you work with competent legal counsel from the inception of your business.

Asset protection also involves maximizing your wealth by minimizing the taxes that you and your business pay. The business owner, if he has an estate-planning attorney, should also include this attorney in the discussion of protecting his personal wealth. Creating a legal entity for the business may be just the tip of the iceberg with respect to asset protection planning. Depending upon the business owner's wealth and current estate plan, the creation of a new legal entity such as a small business could adversely affect his legal needs. Since this would likely be considered a life-changing event by the estate attorney, he should be involved in the discussions regarding the formation of the new legal entity. Perhaps the business owner will need a multitude of legal entities to maximize his legal protection, reduce his estate taxes, and to preserve wealth that he can pass on to his children and grandchildren. For example, perhaps the estate-planning attorney would like to see a

Family Limited Partnership be created to facilitate the transfer of wealth to future generations.

In short, creating a legal entity is not a simple step that can be quickly checked off your "To Do" list for starting a new business by spending $200 to create your company online. We chose to describe the topics of asset protection, asset protection attorneys, estate planning attorneys, charging orders, and the legal protections afforded by a single-member LLC versus a multi-member LLC to stress to the business owner that you *will* benefit from consultations with experts who specialize in each particular legal area. You need to be sure you've covered your bases. You need to give serious consideration to the selection of legal entity and the limited legal liability protection it provides depending upon your current wealth, insurance needs, the potential risks associated with your business, and your personal risk tolerance.

Internal Revenue Code Section 1244

Sec. 1244 allows losses from the sale of shares of small domestic corporations to be deducted as ordinary losses instead of capital losses. If an owned stock qualifies under Sec. 1244, the business owner can deduct up to a maximum of $50,000 on an individual tax return or $100,000 on married filing joint tax returns any losses from the sale of this stock. To qualify as Sec. 1244 stock, certain requirements must be met; these include that the corporation's aggregate capital must not have exceeded $1 million when the stock was issued, the corporation's income must not be have been derived by more than 50% from passive activities, and the individual shareholder must have paid for the stock rather than receiving it as compensation. While there are other tests that must be met, these are beyond the scope of this book—the business owner needs to consult with the attorney handling the stock transactions and his accountant. If Sec. 1244 is available, the owner has nothing to lose by working with his attorney to ensure that the stock issued qualifies as Sec. 1244 stock. If additional capitalization is required in the future, the business owner needs to have a discussion with his business attorney and tax professional to see if the additional shares will qualify as Sec. 1244 stock.

CHAPTER 11

What Type Of Tax Entity Is Best For Your Business?

After they've chosen what type of legal entity will be created, the business owner and his accountant can then select the most appropriate tax entity (ideally working together with legal counsel). For tax reporting purposes, a business can be operated as a sole proprietorship, a partnership or a corporation. You should note that there is no separate LLC tax entity. An LLC as a legal entity is *disregarded* for tax reporting purposes. Because it is a very popular legal entity, let's begin with how LLCs are taxed.

We believe that forming an LLC is preferable to incorporating for reasons stated in the previous chapter. Again, the business owner needs to consult with legal counsel before making this decision. We chose the word "incorporating" rather than using the words "being a corporation" to hopefully minimize confusion, since for tax purposes, an LLC can be taxed as a C or an S Corporation. Thus, even though we currently recommend that new business owners form an LLC over incorporating (as long as your legal counsel concurs), we also recommend that the LLC be taxed as a corporation. Depending upon how many members (owners) form the LLC, an LLC can be taxed as a sole proprietorship, a partnership, a corporate division, a C Corporation or an S Corporation. With so many different tax entities available to businesses using the LLC structure, the importance of the team approach to selecting the legal entity is paramount. The IRS has certain default provisions regarding how LLCs will be taxed. These default tax structures are based on the number of members in the LLC agreement. If an individual owns 100% of the LLC, the IRS default rule is that the single member LLC (SMLLC) will be taxed as a sole proprietorship. However, that taxpayer can elect to be taxed as a corporation when applying for the company's employer identification number. If the LLC has two or more members, it is considered a multi-member LLC (MMLLC). In this case, the IRS tax status of the MMLLC will default to partnership tax status. However, the MMLLC can also elect to be taxed as a corporation when applying for an employer identification number (EIN).

Remember, we hope to provide you with a quick summary explanation of the different types of tax entities. The pros and cons of each kind of tax structure and legal entity would fill an entire book, which is outside our focus for now. Thus, the reader needs to consult with a tax advisor for a more in-depth understanding of each tax entity and their advantages and disadvantages.

This chapter primarily focuses on federal taxes. Because every state's taxation rules differ, it is beyond the scope of this book to address state (and local) taxes. State taxes are very broad, and can include income, franchise, gross receipts, sales tax, and other types. This is just another example of why working with a competent tax advisor is so important to the business owner.

Sole Proprietorship

The most simple tax entity is the sole proprietorship. The business owner has much latitude in what he can call his company. The business does not need to register with the Department of State and can begin business without any red tape.

The business owner reports his business income and expenses on IRS Schedule C, which is part of the IRS Form 1040. There is generally no separate business tax return that has to be filed with the IRS or the state. We say "generally" because Pennsylvania is an example of a state that does require the LLC to file a corporate income tax return to show whether it has a capital stock or franchise tax liability.

Since some jurisdictions have a gross receipts tax or some tax other than an income tax (sometimes referred to as a mercantile or privilege tax), it is always a good idea to check with the local tax authorities and your tax professional about other types of taxes that may be imposed.

If the business owner operates as a single member LLC (SMLLC) and desires to be taxed as a sole proprietorship, the business income and expenses are reported on Schedule C of Form 1040. Thus if you desire to keep tax preparation simple, avoid the filing of a business tax return, and have limited liability protection, the single member LLC may be the legal and tax entity of your choice.

Partnerships

The two most common types of partnerships are the general partnership and the limited partnership. All of the partners of a general partnership are personally liable for the debts of the partnership. In a limited partnership, there can be multiple general and limited partners, but there must be at least one general partner (GP). The limited partners (LP) have limited liability to the extent of their investment in the partnership, and they have no management authority.

A multi-member LLC (MMLLC) is an LLC owned by two or more persons, and it is classified by default as a partnership by the IRS. You can elect to have the legal entity taxed as a corporation by filing Form SS-4.

Partnerships are taxed as a pass-through entity. This means that the partnership itself does not pay (federal) income taxes. The income of the business flows through to the business owner (hence the term "pass-through entity"), where it is reported on the business owner's Form 1040 filed with the IRS. If the partnership operates in several states, the partners may be required to file personal income tax returns in those states, and the partnership may be subject to withholding personal income taxes for its partners.

The partners of a partnership are not allowed to pay themselves W-2 wages. Under certain circumstances, the partnership can pay the partners guaranteed payments. The concept of guaranteed payments is beyond the scope of this book.

All these details show us that there are positive and negative consequences associated with all types of tax entities, which are why it is so important to create your business plan, understand your business, and work in unison with your team of trusted advisors.

C Corporations

The C Corporation is not a pass-through entity. It computes its taxable income and pays income taxes directly to the IRS using IRS Form 1120-C. Thus, at the end of each tax year the corporation's expenses are deducted from its revenues, and if the company generates net income, it pays taxes on this net income figure. If the business owner would like to take out as personal profit some of the cash accumulated in the company, the corporation can issue a dividend distribution to the owner. This distribution is not tax deductible by the company—it is generally considered a taxable dividend distribution to the business owner to the extent there are earnings and profits (E&P) in the corporation. This distribution equates to double taxation, a duplicity long bemoaned by many business owners in the United States. Think about it: the income earned by the C Corporation was subject to a corporate tax; now that you as a shareholder receive that dividend distribution, it is taxed again as dividend income. An explanation of E&P is beyond the scope of this book. Therefore, the business owner of a C Corporation needs to consult with his CPA to plan tax minimization strategies.

Although LLCs are often used to provide business owners with limited legal liabilities, you need to understand that a corporation is a corporation is a corporation. Since LLCs provide limited liability protection, your attorney will likely advise you that the legal liability protection of a C or an S Corporation is the same as an LLC (with the exception of the charging order concept discussed in Chapter 10).

S Corporations

The S Corporation is a pass-through entity that files Form 1120S with the IRS. This means that generally the S Corporation itself does not pay income taxes. The income of the business flows through to the business owner (similar to partnership taxation) and is reported on the business owner's Form 1040 filed with the IRS. The S Corporation avoids the issue of double taxation that falls on C corporations when distributions are made to the shareholders, and it is also a powerful tool that can be used to minimize the payment of FICA and Medicare taxes in certain circumstances. One of the tax negatives of an S corporation is that the benefits (health insurance, etc.) paid to the owner (shareholder) who owns two percent or more of the business is generally considered taxable W-2 wages, whereas these benefits are generally not considered taxable compensation to the C corporation shareholder/employee. If the S Corporation operates in a multitude of states, the shareholders may be required to file individual income tax returns in those states, which increase the cost of compliance for the business owner. Shareholders of C Corporations generally need not file personal income tax returns in every state where the corporation does business, which is an advantage.

Once again, we reiterate that you need to consult with a tax professional about state income taxes. Some state laws have found that if you are an S Corporation for the purposes of federal income taxes, you are automatically treated as an S Corporation in those states. Other states, such as New Jersey, require that a separate tax election be made if a business wants to be treated as an S Corporation in that state. If the business fails to make a timely state election to be taxed as an S Corporation, the business will be treated as an S Corporation for federal income tax purposes and a C Corporation for state income tax purposes. And there are other states, such as New Hampshire, that do not recognize S Corporations. These states treat all corporations as C Corporations.

Owners of S Corporations need to consult with their tax professional to become familiar with the reasonable compensation issue, understand how stockholder basis is computed and why it may prevent losses from the S Corporation to be used currently, and how certain distributions to the shareholder may be tax-free or subject to the capital gains tax.

S Corporation vs. Partnership

While there are similarities between S Corporations and partnerships with respect to them both being pass-through tax entities, there are significant differences that also must be considered when deciding how one wants to be taxed. Whereas S Corporations must pay their employee/shareholder a reasonable salary, which means a payroll processing service is needed, partners do not receive W-2 wages and a payroll service is not needed unless there are non-partner employees who need to be paid. We briefly mentioned that S Corporation shareholders must understand the stockholder basis rules. Likewise, partners must understand how their partnership basis and capital accounts are computed. The partnership computation is different than that of the S Corporation, especially with respect to the liabilities of the business. Whereas all liabilities of the business are generally included when computing a partner's tax basis, the liabilities of the S Corporation are not included in the shareholder's tax basis. The number of S Corporation shareholders is limited, whereas partnerships can have an unlimited number of partners. Another very significant difference is that when distributions are made to corporate shareholders, they must be allocated proportionally among the shareholders. This means that a 60% percent shareholder needs to receive 60% of the distribution, and the 40% shareholder must receive a proportionate share of the distribution. However, when partnerships make distributions to the partners, these do not have to be proportionate to the partners' interests at the time of distribution. Eventually the partnership capital accounts must be trued up, but the partnership rules provide greater flexibility to the owners of the business.

C Corporation vs. S Corporation

As discussed above, a major difference between the two types of corporations exists in how taxes are paid. This difference can perhaps be best explained using a simple example. Assume that the business generated $100,000 of cash revenues and incurred $75,000 of cash expenses that included the owner's salary of $50,000. Thus, the business has net income of $25,000. Let's assume that the corporation retains the remaining $25,000 ($100,000 less $75,000) in its corporate checking account.

If taxed as an S corporation, the corporation pays no federal income taxes. However, taxes still must be paid for those earnings by shareholders. **The S shareholder is taxed on the net income of the S corporation, even though the cash was not distributed to him**. Referring back to our example, this means the shareholder would report a total of $75,000 on his personal return (W-2 compensation of $50,000 plus $25,000 of K-1 income from the S corporation). Again, remember that state and local tax jurisdictions have their own rules, which the owner needs to review with a tax advisor.

The C Corporation is taxed differently. Since the company generated $25,000 of profits, the company (and not the individual) pays income taxes on this amount. The C Corporation shareholder would only report the $50,000 W-2 compensation on his personal income tax return.

You need to remember that when the C Corporation was used, the $25,000 of net profits did not escape taxation—the C Corporation still had to pay taxes on this income. In both scenarios, the owner of the company paid taxes on his W-2 income of $50,000. Taxes on the remaining $25,000 are paid either by the owner (S Corp.), or by the business (C Corp.).

At this point, you may ask yourself why any person would elect S Corporation status, as it appears that the S Corporation owner is reporting an additional $25,000 of income on his personal income tax return.

Think about it this way: When the remaining amount is distributed from the C Corporation to the shareholder (remember, the C Corporation paid taxes on this amount, thus the full $25,000 is not available), this will be considered a taxable event that is reported by the shareholder owner on his personal income tax return (as dividend income). This is where the term "double taxation" comes in; the $25,000 of net profits is taxed at both the corporate level and at the individual level when distributed as a dividend.

But one very important factor when deciding whether to use a C Corporation or an S Corporation is the difference between the marginal tax rates of the C Corporation versus the individual. If the C Corporation were paying income taxes at a 34% tax rate and the individual shareholder/employee were in the 25% tax bracket, the S corporation would be more attractive from a tax perspective. The reverse would hold true if the individual income tax rate was higher than the corporate rate.

One may be inclined to jump to the conclusion that an S Corporation is thus preferable to a C Corporation. After all, who wants to pay taxes twice on the same income! As mentioned above, there are positives and negatives with each type of legal entity. What if we determined that a reasonable salary for the owner was $75,000 and not the $50,000 currently being paid? Then the company's net income is zero and there is no double tax. Furthermore, if the owner is receiving paid benefits from his C Corporation, those would likely be fully deductible by the C Corporation and not be taxed to the owner personally. If an S Corporation were used, the owner would likely have additional taxable compensation to report on his personal income tax return.

Because of the numerous factors that must be considered, this is why we recommend that all of the client's business advisors should be involved when deciding how best to structure the legal entity from both a legal and tax perspective.

The business owner also should be aware that the chance of being audited by the IRS also changes depending upon the type of legal entity. We are not suggesting that a legal entity should be selected based on the likelihood of being examined by the IRS; it is our belief that if the businesses' tax deductions are properly documented and substantiated then it makes no difference if they are audited. However, it is a fact that sole proprietors filing Schedule C have historically been audited by the IRS almost three-times more often than S Corporations and partnerships. We believe the reason for this significant difference is because sole proprietorship are more likely to file self-prepared tax returns, and thus are more likely to make mistakes. The IRS audits those taxpayers where it believes it can get the highest assessments. It is also more likely that business owners who prepare their own tax returns will not pay a professional to represent his interests before the IRS during an audit, meaning that the IRS can more easily disallow deductions and assess additional taxes.

We recognize that the material in this chapter was quite dense, but we gave this information because we believe that choosing the legal entity, asset protection and limited legal liability protection plans for your business needs to be taken very seriously. When you are meeting with your business attorney or asset protection attorney, we hope that you will find this chapter to be a useful guide in your initial discussions.

Hopefully you have learned in this chapter that there is not one particular legal or tax entity that is best for all business owners, but rather

that each individual situation must be analyzed based on the business plan.

Now that you have created your legal entity and you know how you plan to be taxed, what tax account numbers does your business require?

Part Two

Financial Health &

Tax Compliance

CHAPTER 12

What Tax Account Numbers Does Your Business Require?

N ow that you know the legal and tax entity structures of your business, you can begin the process of obtaining the required tax account numbers.

The EIN, or Employer Identification Number, is issued by the IRS. This is likely the most important TIN (taxpayer identification number) that you will need. The form for applying for the EIN is IRS Form SS-4, Application for Employer Identification Number.

When creating a legal entity for a client, some lawyers will automatically file this form for the client. Other attorneys assume that the CPA will do it, since it is an IRS form. You can also file it yourself. In our experience, it is usually best to have the CPA file this form because it is very important that it is completed properly to reflect your desired tax entity. An accountant will not charge very much to do this and the owner can rest assured that the form was properly completed and filed. If the owner prepares the form improperly, the accountant's fees to fix the mistake will be greater.

The SS-4 form asks if the application is for an LLC, and if so, how many LLC members there will be. Remember that an LLC is a legal entity and not a tax entity, so unless tax elections are made to tax the LLC as a corporation, the business will be taxed either as a sole proprietor or a partnership, depending upon the number of members in the LLC. The form then asks the applicant to check one box, with the three most common tax entities for start-ups being sole proprietor, partnership, and corporation. You cannot check a box for LLC because, as you now know, there is no such tax entity as an LLC. When individuals self-prepare the SS-4, the type of tax entity to identify on the form usually presents problems. If you apply for an EIN using your corporate entity, the SS-4 form only has a single box to check—it does not differentiate between a C Corporation and an S Corporation. To file as an S Corp., you must elect to do this later. This brings us to another reason why it makes sense to have a CPA complete the SS-4. If the corporation is going to elect to be taxed as an S Corporation, Form 2553, Election by a Small Business Corporation, must be filed within the first 75 days of the tax year for the election to become effective for that tax year. If the S Corporation election is not made in the initial tax year, it can be made in subsequent tax years during the first 75 days of those tax years. If the business owner, attorney and CPA work as a team, timely tax elections are rarely missed.

If you operate as a sole proprietor or if you are a SMLLC operating as a sole proprietor, the IRS does not require that you obtain an EIN unless you will be hiring employees. While the IRS may not require an EIN, we still recommend that you do so for identify theft prevention purposes. When you operate as a business, your business will undoubtedly be asked to provide its EIN or SSN (social security number) for tax reporting purposes. Rather than providing a third party with your SSN, we believe it is better to provide them with an EIN to better protect your SSN from identify theft. Obtaining the EIN from day one also will avoid future headaches. For example, if you use your SSN and then hire an employee, the IRS will require the use of an EIN, and then you will likely need to notify third parties of the change in the tax identification number, such as your bank, vendors, or parties to whom you supplied a Form W-9.

After you have obtained your EIN, you can open a business bank account. We will discuss this topic in the next chapter when we address the business's accounting needs.

Depending upon the state where your business is located, you may need to apply for a state tax account number. Whereas many states simply use the federal EIN as the state TIN, this is not the case across the board. Some states, such as Pennsylvania, require that the business apply for a separate business account number for reporting state income taxes, employer payroll taxes, sales taxes, and unemployment taxes. In addition, Pennsylvania also has local payroll taxes, so the business will also need to apply for those tax account numbers. The take away here is that by working with a CPA who works with new business owners, you will be sure to obtain the proper tax account numbers and to timely remit your payroll withholdings.

Depending upon the municipality where your business is located or operating, you may be subject to local ordinances regarding zoning and occupancy, as well as local taxes. It is very important to identify these local rules before committing to where your business will operate.

With your tax account numbers now in hand, you are in a position to set up your tax and accounting records. The following chapter will offer suggestions for efficient and organized recordkeeping.

CHAPTER 13

How Does a Business Set-Up Its Tax and Accounting Records?

Bank Accounts

One of the first steps is to open a company business checking account and obtain a business credit card. The bank will need your EIN and perhaps even the company bylaws or operating agreement that authorizes the person opening the bank account to do so on behalf of the business. Accordingly, when forming your legal entity, make sure that the bylaws or operating agreement specifically names the person(s) who are authorized to handle the banking transactions. If the business will be subject to remitting sales and payroll taxes, some business owners may find it helpful to create a separate bank account where these monies can be deposited. This way, the owner need not worry if he has sufficient funds in his regular business checking account to remit the payment of these taxes when due. When choosing the bank that your business will use, one consideration the business owner needs to consider is whether the bank allows a seamless download of your company's banking transactions into your accounting software program. This is discussed in more detail later in this chapter.

Co-mingling of Business and Personal Transactions

Many a new business owner has a difficult time understanding that it is important for tax reporting and for limited legal liability purposes to separate personal financial affairs from the business. Hence, there is a real need for a separate business bank account and credit card. This means the owner pays for all personal expenses with personal funds. Likewise, all business expenditures are made from the business checking account or a credit card in the name of the business. In those rare cases where the business owner cannot obtain a business credit card because of credit or risk concerns, the business owner should devote one personal credit card to the business and be sure to use that credit card <u>only</u> for business transactions. Once the business has established a good credit history and can obtain a credit card in its name, the use of the personal credit card should cease immediately.

This is more difficult to do that you might think. Though it's easy to understand the concept of separating business from personal expenses, some business owners do not follow the practice. Perhaps they believe it makes no difference from which pocket of their trousers payment is made, or in which account a business deposit is made, because they own all of the pockets. We have found this particularly true when working with sole proprietorships, SMLLCs, and single-shareholder S Corporations. In these situations, the business owner believes that since "he *is* the business," he can use the business funds for whatever his personal needs may be. This is a bad practice, and you should be reluctant to do so. **The co-mingling of business and personal transactions needs to be avoided.** Mixing business and personal transactions can create tax and/or legal issues for the owner. If you can't keep business and personal transactions separate, you can create unintentional and adverse tax consequences, including the filing of an incorrect business tax return that underreports your personal compensation from the business, resulting in assessments for underpayment of payroll taxes, or even losing an S Corporation election for disproportionate distributions to the company's shareholders. For example, the single-owner of an S Corporation decides to pay personal expenses using business funds, construing the effect as equal to tax-free withdrawals from the business or as repayment of capital the owner had advanced to the company. However, without proper documentation and substantiation, the IRS may view these payments as disguised compensation and assess penalties for failing to timely remit payroll taxes when due. Proper accounting procedures and substantiation is important when dealing with the IRS.

From a legal perspective, if the owner co-mingles his business and personal funds, he is not respecting the legal entity that was created to provide limited legal liability. If the business owner is not respecting his own legal entity, who can say whether a court will in case the business is sued? Attorneys often refer to this practice as piercing the corporate (or limited liability company) veil. The courts can pierce the veil by finding that the business entity is the alter ego of the individual owning the business. You need to consult with your attorney on matters of this nature.

How to Maintain the Business Books

You have much latitude in how you set up your books and records. While there are IRS requirements as to the methods of accounting (e.g., cash versus accrual) that may be required of certain types of businesses, there are no IRS requirements regarding how you must maintain your books and records. The IRS only requires that you maintain books and records to document and substantiate your business revenues and expenses. This means you can use a software program or maintain your books using paper and pencil and a cardboard box. However, if you fail to properly substantiate your business deductions, you'll lose tax deductions that adversely affect your cash flows, which could subject you to IRS penalties (and of course, these are not tax deductible).

To keep your CPA's fees to a minimum, we recommend that you maintain your books using QuickBooks Pro. While we have no allegiance to QuickBooks and there are other good accounting software products on the market, QuickBooks is the most commonly used software among small business owners. This is why most CPAs use QuickBooks in their own practice. In fact, QuickBooks is so ubiquitous that the IRS now trains its auditors in the software to make the audit exam process more efficient. The program is universally accepted and does a very good job for most business operations. Accordingly, it makes sense to use it in your business. Should you be familiar with another software program and prefer to use it, we recommend that you discuss this with your CPA to make sure it won't make a complicated process even worse when it comes time to do your taxes.

One of the biggest challenges we see in our practice is taking over the tax accounting process from a business that does not use a trained or experienced accountant or bookkeeper. Often we see that the business owner desires to maintain the books himself, or he leaves the details of accounting to a spouse, relative, or friend. This decision is a very bad one if none of these people is a trained accountant. There needs to be someone whose primary responsibility is to be in charge of the accounting records because when the business is started, you are going to have many responsibilities just operating and marketing the business. If you intend to maintain the books yourself, invariably you won't find the time to do so, and the books and records will be ignored.

We believe that most people do not like accounting activities. When running a busy new start-up, they have a tendency to do what they like to do first, and generally they like to do the things that come easy to them and that they are good at. What this means for the accounting records is that they will likely be postponed and ignored. But think about it—is it prudent to have your spouse maintain the financial records and be privy to the financial aspects of your business? Remember that about one-half of marriages wind up in divorce court. If your spouse, relative or friend is not suitably qualified to maintain the books, the only motivating factor to get them involved would be to save money. If you are determined to do the books yourself or if you must have a close acquaintance keep the books, we recommend that you get your accountant set up the chart of accounts in QuickBooks first, then provide training to the person who will be keeping your books. This step is important, as it is not uncommon for new business owners to set up their own chart of accounts and start recording transactions in QuickBooks without any training. This can turn the task into a monumental problem in the future, because the accounting records will have to be redone to correct them.

Some businesses use a proprietary software program to manage their business. For example, a franchisor may require your business to use a networked software program so the parent company can track your revenues and royalty fees due the franchisor. Accordingly, this software package may only track revenues and not expenses. Some companies need a special software package to monitor their inventory, cost of sales, labor, etc. When using such a proprietary software program, be sure to inquire if that software package is compatible with QuickBooks (or whatever software program you are using for recordkeeping). Don't rely on a sales representative who tells you that the software program is supposed to be compatible with QuickBooks. Instead, go to the source. Work with that software company's customer service or technical support to walk you through how you interface or download the data from that program into QuickBooks. Once you've downloaded to QuickBooks, make sure that the downloaded transactions represent your company's actual results. Some programs integrate very smoothly; others do not. For those programs that do not integrate properly, you will end up spending a significant amount of time and money to correct the problems. Some software companies are eager to make a sale to a new business, but as soon as you've paid for their product, they are not as attentive as they should be to correct any issues and problems.

Downloading of Bank and Credit Card Transactions

One of the nice features of an accounting software program is that you can download your bank and credit card transactions from the Internet directly into your QuickBooks (or other software program). This can be a real time saver. For example, assume you have 100 credit card transactions on average each month. Rather than manually inputting these 100 transactions one at a time, you simply download all of the transactions into QuickBooks. The download is completed in a matter of a couple of minutes. One of the built-in features of QuickBooks is that it memorizes the vendor's name, amount and its expense category. So if you pay ABC Property Management Co. each month $500 for your rent expense, the download will automatically show the payment of $500 to ABC as a rent expense.

When selecting the bank for your business checking account and for your credit card, be sure to ask if the bank provides a download service to QuickBooks. Make sure that the person you are speaking with clearly understands that you are asking about QuickBooks and not Quicken. While Quicken is an excellent software program, it is more geared to managing personal finances. We also recommend that the bank representative go online with you (or your accountant) and show you how the QuickBooks download is done. This exercise is not designed to teach you how to do the download, but to verify that the download can be done. This exercise will also inform you whether the download can be made directly from QuickBooks where QuickBooks connects with your bank online, or if you must go online to the bank and download the needed files to your desktop and then upload those Web-connected files into QuickBooks. We have found that both types of downloads work quite well.

While credit card transaction downloads from the bank to QuickBooks work really well, the bank checking account downloads are often more troublesome. We say this because when downloading checks, the download process will insert the check number as the payee name. This means that after the bank download is completed, the person entering these transactions into QuickBooks will need to look at the check images and enter the proper payee and expense category. You won't have this problem when working with ACH debit transactions. Remember—time is money. You may wish to use your credit card or an ACH debit transaction when possible rather than writing a check.

Bank and Credit Card Reconciliations

Regardless of whether the owner, bookkeeper, or accountant is inputting the business transactions into QuickBooks, the bank and credit card accounts must be reconciled each month. Reconciling the accounts provides assurance that all of the deposit and expense transactions in the bank and credit card accounts have been accounted for in your books. When downloading your details from the bank or credit card website, the reconciliation process can be done very efficiently in a matter of minutes.

Credit Card Merchant Services

Your merchant service provider is the company you are using to process credit card payments from customers. How your merchant service provider calculates fees can also create potential problems for your books. Some merchant service providers like to deduct their fees from the sales proceeds collected, and this will generally pose an accounting problem for the business owner. Let's look at an example. Assume that the total credit card sales for the month were $100 and the merchant service fee was 5%. The merchant service provider would deduct the $5 charge from the $100 of receipts and deposit $95 into the business checking account. This $95 deposit on the bank statement will not match the company's revenue reports that show $100 of revenues. While this was a very simple example, the reconciliation problem becomes exponentially greater when you consider that you may have hundreds of sales transactions each month of various amounts. Accordingly when signing a merchant service contract, you want to make sure that the fee is charged separately. This way the business will see $100 being deposited and $5 being withdrawn as a fee. Now the bank deposits will match the sales reports of the company. In addition, the business owner now has a means to track the actual cost of his merchant service fees.

When you use merchant service providers, there will be a time lag from when the company records the sale on its books and when the money is deposited in the business account. Obviously, a shorter period is better for the business owner. Earlier deposits improve your cash flows, which makes reconciling the business bank account easier because there will be fewer deposits in transit at the month end.

Recording of Revenues

You have a responsibility as a business owner to properly track and report your business revenues and expenses. The U.S. tax law is written from the perspective that all revenues are taxable unless specifically exempted by law. We recommend to business clients that they include the underlined text entire amount of monies received from their customers to their business bank account. For example, if the business owner received $2,000 of revenues for the day, deposit the full amount into the business checking account. This discipline allows the CPA and the IRS to match cash revenues generated by your sales system for the day directly to that day's bank deposits. If the business owner only deposits $1,500 in the business account because he kept $500 as a withdrawal, there is a discrepancy between the sales register system ($2,000) and the bank deposit ($1,500). If you need $500 for personal expenses, write a check to yourself for $500 and in the memo section of the check insert something like "withdrawal by owner." This simple step will make bank reconciliations, and reviews by your accountant or the IRS much easier to substantiate.

Recording of Business Expenses

Whereas the U.S. Tax Code is written so that all revenues are taxable unless specifically exempted by law, that same Code states that no business expenses are allowed unless specifically provided for in the Code. We have often been asked by business owners, "What business expenses can I deduct for taxes?" Our response to that question is that the Code is quite broad, so as long as the expenditure is ordinary and necessary to your business, the IRS will allow the expense as a tax deduction. In some cases, the business owner is entitled to a tax deduction in the current year; other times the expenditure must be capitalized (treated as an asset) and depreciated or amortized over several years. An example of the latter would be machinery or equipment (M&E) purchased for the business. While M&E may have to be capitalized and shown as an asset on the company's books, the business owner could depreciate this asset and obtain a tax write-off via the depreciation deduction. Rather than talk in generalities, we recommend to our clients that they record all expenditures in their accounting records. Later, when we review those records, we will make any required adjustments to conform to IRS rules and regulations.

Proper substantiation and documentation will preserve your tax deductions. Even if an expense item is deductible for tax purposes, **the onus is on the business owner to substantiate and document the deduction**. Thus, good record keeping is paramount and the business owner needs to work with the CPA to properly document those tax deductions to withstand IRS scrutiny. Two areas of particular concern we have observed in our tax practice relate to meals & entertainment expenses and vehicle (auto) expenses.

Meals and Entertainment Expenses

Meals consumed by the business owner during the course of the day are generally not tax deductible. Some business owners think that because they eat during the day to attend to business activities, the cost of the meals are tax deductible. To avoid IRS problems, these should not be deducted as business expenses. Generally, the IRS does not allow meals consumed by the business owner or his employees to be deducted unless the business requires that person to be away from home overnight. Meals and entertainment (M&E) expenditures can also be deducted for business purposes if the owner is meeting with clients or prospective clients. Proper documentation for M&E expenditures includes the date of the event, the names and business relationships of the persons involved, the business location, the dollar amount spent, and the business purpose of the event. If the event resulted in a new client, increased billings, a vendor discount or some other benefit to the business, you should document that. Keep in mind that M&E expenses are not fully deductible, but are 50% deductible if properly documented. Accordingly, it is important that M&E expenditures be recorded in a separate general ledger account to keep them separate from 100% deductible expenses. There *are* some types of meal expenditures that are 100% tax deductible. You should also keep a separate ledger for these types of expenditures so as not to lose half of the tax deduction. The types of meals that the business can deduct 100% are beyond the scope of this book, so be sure to discuss this topic with your tax advisor.

Autos and Other Vehicles

If the business uses a vehicle, IRS rules require the user of the vehicle to maintain a **contemporaneous** mileage log that shows the dates traveled, the miles traveled, and the business purpose of each trip. No mileage log book, no tax deduction. This deduction cannot be "put together" at the end of the year by looking at total miles traveled and *estimating* how many pertained to business. Some business owners are under the misconception that they need not maintain a mileage book if they claim actual expenses rather than deducting the flat IRS allowed rate for each business mile. A mileage log book must be maintained for any business owner who claims expenses associated with a vehicle. Since the vehicle will be used for both personal (commuting to and from work and your residence) and business purposes, the mileage log helps the tax preparer compute the percentage of actual vehicle expenses that are tax deductible.

Preparation of Business Tax Returns

While some business owners are tempted to prepare their own business returns, we do not recommend this. The tax laws are complex and a competent tax preparer can significantly reduce the taxes you pay by implementing tax savings strategies and making the proper elections. Fortunately, most owners realize that the Internal Revenue Code and IRS regulations and rulings are complex, and they will engage a CPA to maintain or review the business records and prepare the tax returns required by the IRS and the state jurisdictions where the company is doing business.

Cash versus Accrual

One of the early decisions you need to discuss with your CPA is whether the business will elect to use cash basis or accrual basis accounting. Many small businesses find it easier to understand their business operations using the cash basis. The cash basis method of accounting is fairly simple. The business owner recognizes income when billings are collected and recognizes expenses when the business check is written or paid by credit card. This can create a matching problem of revenues and expenses. For example, you incur expenses today to provide a service to your customer. If the customer does not remit payment when due, you wind up reporting the expenses in one month and reporting the income in a later month when payment is received.

On the other hand, the accrual basis taxpayer recognizes income when the customer is invoiced, not when the billings are collected. Likewise, expenses are recognized when the expense obligation is incurred, such as when an invoice is received from a vendor, not when paid. Depending upon the type of business you are in, your CPA will be able to provide guidance as to which method may be best for your business from a cash flow and tax perspective. Your CPA can also assist you by identifying methods of accounting that the IRS requires for your business. If the business meets certain criteria, the IRS will *require* that the accrual basis be used. In general, larger businesses use the accrual method because they believe that it gives them a better perspective of the financial health of the business. Publicly held companies who report their financial results using generally accepted accounting methods

(GAAP) are required to report on the accrual basis. The IRS does allow businesses to change their method of accounting if certain conditions are met.

Is it possible to use accrual accounting for your investment and debt needs, but report taxes using a cash accounting method, or vice versa? That is a very good question. Although most businesses use the same method of accounting for tax purposes and to report earnings for external financial needs, there are companies that use one method for financial reporting and another for taxes. The IRS is working to make it mandatory that businesses use the same method for book and tax. Of course, your CPA can tell you more about the details.

Financial Statements

Once the company's books have been set up and your business is operating, you either need to learn how to read your financial statements or periodically meet with your CPA to discuss those financial statements. Your business' financial statements are the progress report that shows the company's financial health. When you understand the financial health of your company, you will be better positioned to effectively manage the business.

We have found in our practice that business owners generally do not have the time to read financial statements, and if they do take the time, they struggle to interpret the results. This is understandable, because many business owners do not have an accounting background. We suggest that you review your financial information monthly with your CPA to get insights about developing trends in your business, and to find ways to increase cash flows. We provide our own clients with what we call "Points of Interest" ("POI"). The POI explains in plain English the ramifications of the business' current financial statements; and we alert our clients of any favorable or unfavorable trends as well as how the business is doing compared to industry standards. This allows the business owner to understand what the business is doing from our perspective as CPAs in a matter of minutes. This is a valuable service. It's one thing to keep good records, but it is difficult to interpret those numbers without an expert to guide you as the numbers develop. You should have a monthly review of your business financial statements with your CPA to verify and measure actual results against the expected results.

The three major financial statements are the balance sheet (statement of assets, liabilities and equity), the income statement (statement of revenues and expenses) and the cash flow statement. The key concepts of each of these statements are addressed below.

The balance sheet shows the assets (cash, receivables, property and equipment, etc.) owned by the company, the debt or liabilities it owes others (payroll taxes due, accounts payable, bank loans, etc.), and the net capital (equity) invested in the business. Accountants are familiar with the equation of $A - L = E$. The equity of the business (E) is equal to the difference between the assets (A) and liabilities (L) of the business. A balance sheet reflects those items on a specific date. For example, a balance sheet as of December 31, 2013, reflects the company's financial position as of that date. Theoretically, there is a different balance sheet for every day of the calendar year. The amounts shown on the balance sheet are usually original cost figures and do not represent fair market value. Accordingly, the owner needs to understand that the equity does not represent the fair market value of the business, but is merely the book value of the business expressed in accounting terms.

The income statement is also referred to as the net profit or loss (P&L) statement (and at times as a statement of revenues and expenses). An income statement is for a period of time which could be for a day, a week, month, quarter or year. The income statement reflects how profitable the company is for the period being reported.

Of the three statements, we believe that the cash flow statement is the most important. It needs to be reviewed by the business owner no less often than monthly. Depending on the business and its cash inflows and outflows, some businesses need to review this statement daily, weekly or even by the hour. The cash flow statement shows by line item the cash coming into the business and the cash leaving the company, the beginning cash balance, the ending cash balance, and the net change in cash for the time period being reviewed. Naturally it is best that the company is showing positive cash flows rather than negative cash flows. However, for a new business just getting started, it is not uncommon for the business to have negative cash flows in the early months. Once the actual cash flows are reviewed, it is an excellent time to compare the business's actual monthly cash flows against those that were projected in the business plan. Don't forget that the business plan included a cash flow projection that identified the total capital needed to fund the business to profitability. If the actual cash flows are worse than those in the budget, management may need to take corrective action as soon as it is apparent to avoid running out of capital.

Accounts Receivables

The business owner needs to frequently review the company's Aged Accounts Receivables Report. When a customer does not pay in full for a service or product, the customer owes the business the balance due. QuickBooks shows the aging of the balance due of current receivables in time periods, such as: 30 days old or less, 30 to 60 days old, 60 to 90 days old, etc. Business statistics show that the longer the account is outstanding (has not been paid), the smaller the likelihood the business will be able to collect the balance due. As a consumer, you likely have noticed that when you work with an attorney, he requires a retainer. Your physician wants immediate payment. When your HVAC contractor services your heating system, the technician will likely immediately process your credit card payment or accept your check for payment. All of these businesses are maximizing cash flows, minimizing uncollectible accounts and reducing the extra work of billing. You should be doing the same in your business whenever market conditions permit you to do so.

What Should the Business Owner Focus On?

We advise our business clients to focus primarily on four things. These are: (1) to thoroughly understand the sources and outflows of the business' cash (the cash flow statement); (2) to not maintain excess inventories; (3) to thoroughly understand the gross profit margins for each of their products, which will help maximize cash flows and profits; and (4) to know and understand the metrics (factors) that drive their business' cash flows and profits. You can't go to any fast food store in America and order a hamburger without being asked if you want fries and a drink. Yes, the counter clerk is being courteous. More importantly, they have been trained to "upsell" products that cost the business very little but return a significant profit margin. It is surprising how many business owners have no idea as to what their gross profit margin is on each product sold or service offered by them. If a customer is undecided between two products that both meet the customer's needs, why not sell the product that has the highest gross profit margin to maximize your cash flows?

There are business owners who place too much emphasis on sales volume or dollar revenues as the primary indicator of the success and growth of their business. If sales volume is increasing, is the business not growing? The problem with this question is where the emphasis is placed. Rather than on sales volume, the emphasis should be placed on the profitability of the business. Obviously if your business has only one product, you are not concerned about product mix. However for businesses with multiple products or services, the owner must thoroughly understand the marginal or incremental profit margin for each product or service offered. Low profit margin products may be necessary as part of your business's inventory if the consumer expects it to be available; those low-margin products help to pay the rent each month and thus cannot be excluded. However, it you want to increase your company's cash flows, product mix economics will teach you to focus on the sales volume of each specific product offered. Thus, rather than merely focusing on increasing overall revenues, it is far more prudent to focus on increasing revenues on those products that have the higher profit margins (such as those sodas and fries we mentioned earlier).

We are going to share a quick story with you. I was advising an electrical contractor who had been in business for several years. Our CPA service offered him a free tax consultation; we would review his personal and business tax returns, look at his company's current financial statements, ask him a few questions, and in 30 to 45 minutes we would let him know if he was overpaying his taxes. Plus, we would allow him to ask us any tax or business question he had without any cost or obligation to him. We thought that this offer was sure to be accepted, as the contractor had nothing to lose. He asked us how much we thought we could save him in taxes. After responding that it would be impossible to predict the overpayment based on our ten-minute telephone conversation, we added that in similar situations we were able to annually save the business owner at least $3,000 in taxes. What was the business owner's response? He told us that it was not worth an hour of his time to meet with us. Wow, we didn't realize that electricians charged $3,000 an hour. But, the story gets better. About two weeks later, we called the electrical contractor back and told him that we were having our entire business rewired. We had received an estimate for $50,000 but wanted to get another estimate. We asked if he could recommend an electrical contractor to us. He quickly offered to provide us with that estimate. We told him that we were confused. Wasn't he too busy to work for less than $3000, we asked? "When we spoke about two weeks ago, you told us that you were too busy to meet with us to discuss how we could save you $3,000 in taxes." The electrician quickly responded: "Yes, I recall saying that. However, that was for $3,000 not $50,000. I will be glad to meet with you for $50,000." But in fact, that $50,000 was actually only worth $3,000 in net profit, based on our previous conversation with the electrician about his business metrics. *It was the same thing.* We explained the interesting news to the electrician. We ran through the gross profit and his net profit margins, explaining how much of the $50,000 contract price actually goes into his bank account. In other words, the $50,000 in revenues, after paying for the cost of materials and labor and his overhead charges plus income taxes, was in fact worth a profit of $3,000. This is a good example of the business owner needing to understand the metrics that drive his profits and cash flows.

We had another client tell us that he had paid $20,000 in advertising fees to generate $30,000 in sales. He was happy with this, because he figured he'd earned an extra $10,000 from this relationship. He planned to pay for more advertising, expecting that it would "finally make him financially successful." It actually pained us to tell him that if he continued to operate this way, he would eventually be bankrupt. The client was astonished and thought that we had not heard him correctly, repeating that he'd paid $20,000 to advertise and generated $30,000 in sales; thus he generated $10,000 of cash for his business. But he'd ignored an important fact: his gross profit margin was 40%. This is not even close to 100%. Thus, the $30,000 in sales would net him $12,000 of gross profits ($30,000 times 40%) after his cost of materials and labor. This didn't even cover the advertising fees of $20,000—the business was generating a negative cash flow of $8,000.

We have countless similar stories of business owners who needed help with their finances as they ran their businesses. We believe it was important to share those two stories with you to illustrate how important it is to understand the financial aspects of your business.

You must block off an appropriate amount of time to review the financial health of your business with your CPA. You may need the assistance of a CPA initially, but over time, you will learn how to read financial statements yourself, and you'll gain a sense of how to react to the information gleaned to make the best business decisions for your growing company.

CHAPTER 14

How to Avoid IRS Tax Problems

We spend a significant part of our tax practice representing individual and business taxpayers with IRS tax debts to get them into compliance with their income tax filings by paying their past-due tax liabilities. For those business owners who timely pay their taxes, they will find most of this chapter irrelevant. However, we know that there are many business owners who have tax problems and therefore decided it was important to include this chapter.

Many individuals had no problems with paying taxes until they began their own business. What often happens is that the business owner becomes fully involved with the various challenges of starting a new business and he doesn't make the time to take care of the financial aspects of the business. We've already discussed that these situations can arise if the owner does not work closely with a tax professional and tries to do everything himself. Every day, it's the same thing: he will address the financial issues tomorrow. Of course, tomorrow arrives and the financial aspects of the business are pushed back to the next tomorrow. Remember, people like to work on what they enjoy doing the most. Financial statements and taxes are at the very bottom of the list of things that many people enjoy addressing. Eventually, all of your tomorrows will become yesterdays, and you'll receive a letter from the IRS notifying you that your business is missing a tax return. Realizing that nearly any letter you might receive from the IRS will be bad news, you don't even open the envelope. This can go on for some time before the pain gets strong enough that you need professional help. We refer to this strategy as the ostrich approach. You have to recognize that burying your head in the sand won't make the problem will go away. When the IRS is involved, it will only make the problem worse. While the IRS is a very slow-moving bureaucracy, it *will* eventually take action, and when it acts, the IRS is the most powerful collection agency in the world.

Let's look at some of the possible mistakes that a business owner who fails to pay adequate attention to tax responsibilities may be making:

- Maintaining inadequate books and records. Not only does the business owner have no idea about how much money the business has at any given time, but he also has no records to give an accountant to prepare the business tax return. This means fewer deductions and more taxes.
- The business that fails to file its tax returns will eventually receive an IRS notice. For a partnership or an S-Corporation, the IRS penalty for failure to file a timely tax return is $195 per month *per shareholder or partner* for each month *or portion of a month* that the return (Form 1120S or Form 1065) is filed late. The penalty assessment is up to 12 months. So if a partnership fails to file its tax return within the first 12 months of its due date (including extensions), the IRS minimum penalty would be $4,680 ($195 per month * 12 months * 2, since a partnership must have a minimum of two partners). You see how quickly this can get out of hand ...
- And it's not over yet! There are other taxes to take into consideration: Once the business return is filed, the small business owner is also required to file a personal tax return, and along with that he must pay 15.3% of Social Security and Medicare self-employment taxes. These payroll taxes are discussed in more detail below.
- Considering all this, let's assume that the small-business owner who didn't plan ahead cannot afford to pay taxes, or simply decides not to. The IRS penalty for filing a personal

tax return late is 5% of the tax due per month for the first five months. Thus, the tax assessment has grown by another 25%. This business owner would have been much better off filing the tax return without the full payment to avoid this costly penalty for failure to file.

- If the business owner does not file his personal tax return, the IRS may prepare the return for him. The IRS calls this a "substitute for return" (SFR). When the IRS computes the tax due, it does so in the least beneficial manner for you; the tax is levied on gross income with the only the standard deduction.

- If the owner is not filing a tax return, it's nearly certain he's not paying any estimated taxes beforehand. This is also a costly mistake: the IRS penalty for failure to timely pay the tax liability is 0.05 percent per month of the tax due (not to exceed 25% of the tax liability).

- To top it all off, the IRS charges you interest on any unpaid taxes as well as on any penalties due.

Don't forget that your business may be required to file taxes for the states in which it operates, and these states will also be assessing interest and penalties for unpaid or unfiled taxes.

We've seen business owners procrastinate for a multitude of tax years; and the problem continues to grow until the IRS has no alternative but to place a lien against the assets of the business owner, garnish wages, or levy bank accounts. The IRS could eventually take steps to close the business down.

Some readers may be thinking this must be an unrealistic scenario that could not happen in the real world. Unfortunately, they are wrong: **This is a <u>very common situation</u> in which the business owner will find himself when he ignores filing business and personal income tax returns on a timely basis.** It is a matter of priorities. Many a business owner will ignore the financial aspects of the business because he is completely overwhelmed with day-to-day burdens of keeping the business afloat. **What the business owner MUST do is to devote a set amount of hours each day or week to address finances. As a small-business owner, you**

must set aside these designated hours on your calendar and do your best to live by that.

Payroll Taxes: It is possible that payroll taxes are the greatest challenge facing the business owner. Even in situations where the owner is diligent in filing his personal income tax return, he may find the tax liability to be greater than he can afford. As a sole proprietor or partner, the business owner is not only responsible for income taxes, but also payroll taxes for Social Security and Medicare. If you've ever worked for a paycheck, you will remember that these payroll taxes were deducted from your earnings each and every week. As a self-employed business owner, the taxes are not deducted automatically—it's the owner's responsibility to deduct them from all employee paychecks and to pay his estimated taxes. If the business owner is in a 25% tax bracket and owes 15.3% for self-employment taxes, the federal tax liability can be significant.

How do we as small-business owners and CPAs who advise our clients avoid this situation? It is really quite simple. The business owner must ask the CPA to prepare quarterly IRS and state estimated tax vouchers for him. The CPA should already be reviewing the financial transactions with the business owner on a regular basis. So the CPA will use that same financial information to prepare estimated tax vouchers. The IRS requires individuals to pay their estimated taxes (income and payroll) on April 15, June 15, and September 15 of the current year, along with another payment due January 15 of the subsequent year. In our experience, some individuals find it difficult to pay quarterly tax payments because they haven't mustered the discipline to set funds aside from all revenues. In situations like this, we suggest paying your estimated tax payments on a *monthly* basis. There is no rule that prohibits you from paying the IRS the estimated taxes of the business more often than required by law. We often recommend this strategy to business owners whose earnings or revenues are received infrequently. For example, a realtor gets paid when the commission is received at closing. If the realtor pays an appropriate amount of estimated tax immediately when the commission is paid, he'll avoid the situation where all commissions earned have been spent by the time the quarterly estimated tax payment is due.

The choices are quite simple. Picture yourself ignoring your estimated tax responsibilities: owing significant taxes, interest and penalties to the IRS, having collection problems such as IRS liens placed against personal residences or other real estate holdings (and seeing such liens recorded for public view at the local county courthouse), even personal bank accounts levied by the IRS. Picture yourself paying significant professional fees to have a qualified tax debt problem resolution specialist represent you before the IRS. Not a pretty picture, is it?

On the other hand, picture yourself prepared and organized, using financial discipline to file and remit estimated tax payments to the IRS and the state income tax authority on a monthly or quarterly basis. Picture you running a successful business; knowing at all times what your cash flows and expenses are, with a professional CPA advising financial matters, and sleeping easily at night because the IRS is far away from your business operations.

Fiduciary Tax Withholdings: Businesses that have employees are required to withhold payroll taxes and to timely remit those taxes. Likewise, businesses that have any sales revenues subject to state sales tax are required to collect those taxes and timely remit them to the taxing jurisdiction. We refer to these as fiduciary taxes because the business owner is placed in the role of collecting these taxes on behalf of the government and remitting them by the due date.

Some businesses experience a temporary cash flow problem. The cash crunch could be due to a payment from a key customer not being received when expected, an unexpected and significant capital repair, or just a bad month where sales were less than expected. The business owner needs to pay his employees and vendors to remain in business. How will your business meet its cash flow needs? We promise you're not the first business owner who is tempted to use sales tax and payroll tax withholding revenues to meet the immediate cash flow needs of the business. Sure, you understand that the withheld taxes are not your money, but cash flows will improve next month and you'll pay the taxes due at that time. This is an easy and temporary fix and all will turn out well. Right?

Perhaps. However, what often happens is that the temporary cash flow problem turns out not to be just a one-off event. The owner now finds himself using the withheld taxes on a continuing basis until the business improves. Think back to the list of tax issues above—remember how quickly those IRS assessments added up? In fact, the penalties associated for failure to timely remit payroll taxes can get severe (the IRS has a 100% penalty that it will impose). Don't let yourself get painted into this corner. If you envision this kind of situation affecting your business in the future, work closely with your accountant *today* to come up with a plan. One such remedy might be securing an emergency line of credit for use only during a short-term cash crunch.

When attempting to recover the unpaid taxes, the IRS will assess taxes, interest and penalties against every person in the business deemed to be responsible for remitting the taxes. Thus, it is possible that the IRS will pursue the collection of payroll taxes against any key officers of the business, as well as employees involved in the payroll process—even the bookkeeper!

Tax Documentation: Business owners need to work carefully with their accountant to ensure that systems are set up to provide a means to substantiate and document tax records. We discussed the importance of this in an earlier chapter in regard to documenting your revenue, expenses, and deductions.

Cash transactions: Some business owners mistakenly pay individuals for their services in cash without reporting the cash payments. We've all heard the term "paying employees under the table." It describes the hidden economy where individuals and businesses fail to report cash receipts for goods, labor, or services. What is the source of the funds used by the business owner to pay others "under the table"? The funds usually come from the revenues generated by the business. If these are revenues reported as sales by the company on its tax return, the business owner has a non-tax deductible business expense. Compounding the problem is when the business owner receives cash for his services or product and does not include these revenues on the tax return. This strategy is fraught with penalties, both civil and criminal, and as a business owner you should avoid it. Keeping your transactions on the up and up will bode well for the long-term outlook for your business.

There are some industries where paying employees under the table is common, practically "de rigueur." Restaurant owners, in particular, have told us that when they hire servers, cooks, or kitchen help from other restaurants, the new hires are surprised when they're asked to fill out a Form W-2. Every restaurant where they've ever worked has paid them under the table. Though this is a common occurrence in some areas, we would exhort you to always document your employees' wages. Why would you jeopardize your personal and business reputation, risk bad publicity, and court public embarrassment in your community for you or your family members if the situation turns into a legal or criminal issue?

Independent Contractors: When analyzing employee costs, which can include workers compensation insurance, unemployment insurance, employer contributions to Social Security and Medicare taxes, employee benefits, and regulatory compliance, just to name a few factors, it's understandable that business owners will look for an alternative.

There are two types of workers—employees and independent contractors. Independent contractors are not entitled to any employer benefits and are responsible for paying their own self-employment taxes (Social Security and Medicare). Recently, more and more business owners are simply calling workers independent contractors as a way to avoid employee costs. This can be a way to cut down on labor costs, but unfortunately for you as a business owner, there is a long history of IRS rulings and case law that determines quite specifically who can be an independent contractor. As an employer, you are not involved in the decision—you cannot just wave the magic wand and say, "Poof! I declare you an independent contractor." The IRS and the Department of Labor have stepped up their audit programs in recent years to identify employers who strategically and consistently misclassify their workers as independent contractors to escape employee costs. Along with the audit program will come civil penalties, as well as extra taxes and interest assessments for misclassifying these workers.

Be very careful about this practice, and be sure to speak with your accountant and business attorney if you believe you can classify some employees as independent contractors. Get an informed opinion to back up your belief before you get yourself into deep water by thinking you can get away with it.

CHAPTER 15

Ten Key Financial Mistakes You Need To Avoid!

Realizing that for most business owners, time is the most precious commodity, we thought it would be relevant to summarize some key financial mistakes to avoid.

1. Starting the business without a comprehensive business plan.
2. Losing valuable tax deductions due to inadequate tax recordkeeping.
3. Failure to analyze your business metrics in detail. You must know which product or service yields the greatest profits and cash flows to the business.
4. Not billing promptly. If you follow up quickly to demand payments due from late paying clients, you will accelerate your incoming cash flows and reduce the likelihood of uncollectible accounts.
5. Extending credit to customers with credit risks. Always perform credit checks to minimize uncollectible accounts. When working with risky accounts, be sure your potential reward is commensurate with the credit risk.

6. Refusing to pay for professional help. Remember to focus on the value of benefits and services received from your professional partners, not on the face cost of those services. Sometimes it can save you money to pay a lawyer or a tax advisor.

7. Disregarding the financial results of your business for too long. You cannot steer a ship without a lookout—be sure to pay regular attention to the trends of your cash flows and other finances so that corrective action may be taken if an unfavorable trend is developing.

8. Failing to meet regularly with your CPA to evaluate how the business is doing; also, hiding or not sharing important financial details of your business and personal accounts with your CPA.

9. Ignoring basic IRS rules and requirements because you imagine that you'll never be audited or interpreting the rules according to your needs without first consulting your CPA to be sure your methods will stand scrutiny. Remember, you must not allow your anger or sense of injustice about tax laws to color your decisions in this area. A successful business will find a way to make it work legally. An unsuccessful business will not last through its first audit.

10. Stretching tax due dates, making late tax status elections, filing returns and remitting taxes after the deadline. For whatever the reason, you must prepare and think ahead to make these deadlines. IRS punishments can be merciless if your business misses deadlines and begins to pile up late fees and tax debts.

CHAPTER 16

The Home Office

Since many new businesses operate from homes to conserve cash, or establish a home office for tax reasons, we thought it best to include a chapter about the tax implications of home offices. Before we begin, however, I feel I must offer an anecdote that betrays my thinking on the issue.

I had a conversation with a fellow CPA who shared the following story with me. A business owner who had about a dozen stores and was looking for a new CPA had given him a call. After a lengthy discussion about the owner's needs, both parties agreed that it was worth a face-to-face meeting, so an appointment was set to meet at the CPA's place of business. The CPA told me that he had looked forward to the meeting because his business was just getting started, and securing this business-owner for a client would quickly jump-start his practice. But on the date of the meeting, the business owner drove to the address and was confused by the location, which was located in a neighborhood of family homes. After reaching the CPA for directions, the business owner learned that he was not lost but was just a couple of minutes away from the CPA's home office. Needless to say, the business owner never arrived. Upon learning that the CPA worked from his home, the businessman explained that he was no longer interested in working with the CPA. He needed a CPA who had a full-time practice, he said.

This is just a single story, we admit, but it does illustrate the mental impression that a home office location gave to that potential client when he was searching for a professional CPA.

Why did we share this story with you? We believe that if your business is offering almost any kind of professional services, you may face the same problem. As a new business start-up, you have to decide for yourself: do you incur the expense of leasing office space, or do you work from your home? We asked ourselves this same question 14 years ago when we started our tax practice. We have never regretted our decision to lease professional office space. Obviously there is no single correct answer to this question, so the choice must be yours.

We admit freely that it is possible to run a professional business from your home. Some professional service providers, to avoid the type of reaction that the CPA above received, could offer to meet at the customer's place of business. The information technology industry has many business owners who have found this approach works well for them. Another option is to offer to buy breakfast for your client and meet at a local diner or restaurant. Although the ability to speak freely in a public setting could possibly be a concern, the thinking here is that once a business relationship is created, your client will become comfortable with the quality of service provided. If you have the type of business that allows you to build a trusting relationship, your customer will not care where your business is located.

Other business owners solve the problem by working from a virtual office. A virtual office space is a large space shared by many smaller businesses that all have access to the basic amenities a larger company would pay for by itself. These companies will rent a fully equipped office with no up-front capital. These amenities include a receptionist to answer your phone with personalize greetings, personal office space, access to high-speed Internet and computer equipment including printers, faxes, copiers, and other business tools, and larger meeting space such as a conference room for presentations and meetings. You can rent by the day, week, month or year. In other words, you can get a very professional office setting that fits within your budget and provides you with great flexibility. One such company we know in the Philadelphia area is called Regus. According to their website, this company has over 1500 virtual office locations in 600 cities around the world. There are other virtual office companies, as well.

We have known financial advisors who used this approach. For example, they may conduct a seminar and explain to their participants that they have offices in five different cities for their client's convenience. In reality, these advisors have only one office location, but they will rent virtual office space for a day at a time for the convenience of their prospective customers. In this way, the advisor makes it more convenient to meet clients in person, and have thus eliminated one reason that might prevent a potential client relationship. Once this financial advisor secures a client and begins to cement the relationship based on quality work, mutual trust and interdependency, the client will likely have no issue with traveling a longer distance to meet in the future.

For those business owners who find that working from their personal residence meets their business needs, they need to discuss with their tax professional the details of claiming a home office on their personal tax return. If a portion of the personal residence (including apartments or other rented properties) is used regularly and exclusively for business purposes and is the principal place of business, then certain expenses are allowable as a business expense. Usually the portion of the residence that is used for business is determined by dividing the square footage of the space used for the business (this can be less than a full room) by the total square footage of the residence. This percentage can then be applied to costs associated with your property rental or mortgage, such as real estate taxes and mortgage interest (which are normally deductible only as an itemized deduction on IRS Form Schedule A). Your home office deductions may also be applicable against related costs that aren't normally deductible for business reasons. These may include homeowner's insurance, rent, certain repairs and maintenance, security systems, utilities, and depreciation.

Beginning in 2013, the IRS allows a simplified alternative for computing home office deductions. Again, you should discuss with your tax professional to determine if you should elect this alternative method. While the amount of recordkeeping may be simplified, this alternative method may allow a smaller total deduction, which would make it less attractive. Another consideration is that some states, such as Pennsylvania, do not accept the IRS simplified method.

No matter which method you use for your home office, there are special rules that may limit the tax deduction, such as the amount of net income that the business is generating. Working with a tax professional to claim a home office is important, particularly because your chances of an IRS audit are increased when you claim a home office deduction. Again, documentation is always the key to substantiate any tax deduction claimed.

Part Three
Growing Your
Business

CHAPTER 17

Is Marketing Important To Your Business?

The answer to that question is quite simple. You bet it is! It is very important no matter what your specialty or field.

For example, we provide financial services to our clients. We have experience, training, and expertise in the financial aspects of running a successful business. Even so, we do not think we're prejudiced when we say that making good choices about the financial aspects of your business is one of the most important aspects to your success. However, after saying this, we have to admit that our specialty might come in a close second to another important factor—having an effective marketing strategy in place. Effective marketing brings revenues to your business; and without revenues, no financial analysis is needed. Your business won't need an accountant, because there will be nothing to count!

While you may have started your own business so you could "work for yourself," any successful business owner knows the real reason for coming to work: it's your customers. If your business does not provide a benefit or address the needs of your customers, then another business will get their money. On the other hand, the more people who need your product or service, the more revenues you will generate. So if your business sees declining revenues, rather than asking yourself the question "How can I increase these dang revenues?"; you might want to turn the question on its head and ask yourself how you can better help others. People don't buy from you because they like you; they buy from you because you are satisfying a need. So think of marketing not just as a matter of generating more sales but as giving your customer a compelling reason to buy from you.

To cover all the aspects of effective marketing is beyond the scope of this book. However, due to its great importance, we think it's imperative to mention some key aspects of marketing. We realize we're only touching the tip of the iceberg. As you've noticed with our earlier thoughts on using professional advisors, we believe it's important to match the needs of your business with expert help. We are not marketing experts, our knowledge of start-up business financial matters and tax-saving practices notwithstanding. Accordingly, we also recommend that the business owner go to more than one source to find marketing advice. Read popular books on marketing, engage an experienced marketing consultant, and ask your local SCORE office to set you up with a marketing-experienced mentor, if possible. You should never underestimate how helpful your local SCORE office can be!

Key marketing aspects include:

1. Target your audience by using the right channels. Do not market to everyone; market only to your ideal customer. Marketing costs money, so it makes sense that customer acquisition should be as efficient as possible. With the necessarily limited resources of your start-up business, you need to devote research to the best channels that will reach your customers. To do this, you'll also need to know who you're looking to target, which leads us to the next step.

2. Identify who is your business's ideal customer (or client). Start with the general and move toward specific. Are you targeting business-to-business (B2B) or individual consumers? For example, we know of a financial advisor who targets individuals who have come into a significant sum of money. They may have won the lottery, a court judgment, or

an inheritance, and need guidance as to how to invest their newly acquired wealth. This advisor receives much personal satisfaction helping these people preserve and growth their wealth. Equally as important is that these people truly appreciate what he does for them.

3. Identify the wants and needs of your ideal customer. If your start-up is an existing business, you can take a focused look at who makes up your current ideal customer base by interviewing your clients. What are their needs? Why did they decide to do business with you? What do they find unique about your business that they can't find elsewhere? Are there changes to your offerings that they would like to see? What aspects of your business would they prefer to remain the same?

4. Identify where you can find this ideal customer. When you know exactly where your customer can be found, you can better market to them. This may be as simple as becoming familiar with the demographics of your local areas by ZIP code. If you wish to market to wealthy individuals, individuals of a certain educational background, age bracket, or marital status, you can. Information about how to reach these specific consumers is readily available. For example, if you want to market to equestrian riders, you might find out what periodicals they read, where they spend their days riding, and the names of area veterinarians who specialize in treating horses. Are the numbers of facilities in your area where owners board their horses growing, declining, or ... stable? (Pardon us; we couldn't help a good pun!) These are just to name a few ideas.

5. Compute the number of ideal customers in the geographic area your business will service. Are there a sufficient number to sustain your business? Is the number growing? Declining? Stable? If you've done your due diligence before starting or expanding your business, this information should be readily available in your business plan as well.

6. Identify the decision makers who buy from you and how they make their decisions. What are their motivations? How

do you attract these decision makers? It has been said that customers buy for one of two reasons: either for fear of loss or hope of gain. In other words, customers do not buy your product or service. Rather, they buy what your product or service will do to solve their problems. They want the benefits you can provide or the solution to their problem. Good marketing focuses on the benefit, not the product.

7. Identify your USP or UVP (unique selling or value proposition) to distinguish you from everyone else who offers the same service or product. Some people refer to this as finding your market niche. You need to separate your business from the crowd. Be careful of adopting marketing clichés such as "We offer quality service" and "We care about you." These hackneyed phrases have saturated our consumer society to the point that they don't mean anything anymore. Unfortunately, they will not differentiate your business from your competitors. Do you really think your target customer believes your company is the only business that offers quality service or cares about its customers? Of course not. Make your message mean something based on research and reality.

A marketing consultant we respect has told us before that "every business owner is in the business of show business" to some extent. To market your business, you need step into the spotlight and show off the features that make your business stand out and give it a star quality. Being the best in your business might not be good enough—in many cases, being different will sell more widgets than being good. The marketing plan for your business should speak to your ideal customer and hold his attention. This is where it becomes important to know your unique selling proposition and to market it using a perceived brand that the ideal customer can come to know because it satisfies a recurring need.

8. Be careful about marketing yourself as the face of your business. Although you may be the one who eventually gives service, your ideal customer likely is not interested in learning about you. This is America, land of capitalism, where every

person can hang a shingle—thus, there are nearly always a multitude of service providers who offer the same service (or product) you do. Begin to build a brand and a history of service or quality. Your business itself will acquire a reputation that will represent itself for you.

9. Realize that seducing the ideal customer to become an actual customer of your business can be a long and arduous journey. You may need to keep in constant contact with your target audience for an extended time until the moment your product or service is needed, and increase the chance that your potential customers will think of you first.

Search on the Internet for the phrase "How many touches does it take to make a sale?" You will see that the consensus is that it takes 7 to 13 touches to make a sale. Too many business owners quickly give up on marketing efforts when the prospect does not immediately become a customer. For example, a single direct mailing or email blast may return very disappointing results (getting new customers). A less-informed marketer might quickly abandon that mode of advertising, saying that it doesn't work. A study by the National Sales Executive Association (NSEA) found that there is a direct correlation between the number of "touches" and the percentage of prospects converted to a sale. Here's what the NSEA found:

- 2% of sales are made after the first contact
- 3% of sales are made after the second contact
- 5% of sales are made after the third contact
- 10% of sales are made after the fourth contact
- **80% of sales are made between the fifth and twelfth contacts**

As my good friend and marketing consultant Michael Rozbruch says, *The really sad part is that most professionals are leaving 98% of the sales on the table because they stop communicating with their prospects after only one contact! Most firms average a conversion rate of more than 5% but less than 10% of the total number of leads that walk in their door. The ability to increase the conversion rate is in direct proportion to their willingness to increase the number of touches they make to their prospects.*

It takes time to build credibility and trust with your customers. A business relationship is not much different than that of building a personal relationship. If you are fortunate enough to find the woman of your dreams and ask her to marry you on your first date, it's fairly certain you're going to be disappointed. However, if you enter into a courtship with her, the likelihood that she will realize that you are someone she wants to engage will increase over time. During the courtship, you may occasionally give her flowers, a box of candy, treat her to a movie or play she wants to see, or dine at her favorite restaurant. It is all about developing a relationship. Marketing to consumers is no different. Your target consumer does not know you and will likely not respond to a single advertising piece. However, if the consumer sees your ad every month for several months, your business earns a place in your customer's mind as a place he'll think of first. If your business can provide something of value to the customer with each of those contacts, so much the better. For example, a dentist could send a monthly postcard or newsletter describing new dental procedures to make your dental visit more comfortable, new teeth-whitening techniques, and the latest treatment advances to prevent dental problems. The strategy is not that you are selling something, but that you want to share something of value with the ideal customer. The target customer begins to associate your outreach with something of value rather than a sales pitch.

Know, Trust, Try and Buy. This old marketing adage explains the customer relationship process. People buy from people they trust, but to obtain that trust, they must first know you. By introducing yourself to your customer, you begin the process of building a relationship with your target client. If you can follow up and continue to provide value to the prospect without necessarily selling something, the target customer can feel a sense of trust. Eventually the hope is that your target will investigate, give your business a try, and then buy something from you.

Continuous marketing means that your customer will think of you when the need for your product or service is needed. The target customer is not going to remember your business if you sent a single flyer out to his neighborhood six months ago. However, if you can catch that ideal customer with targeted marketing over an extended period of time, the chances of the customer remembering your business and contacting you increases significantly.

10. Know how your customer found you. If you don't ask how your customer found you, you will never find out which form of advertising is working for you.

Effective advertising rarely comes free or cheap. Small businesses are constantly trying to attract customers using various forms of advertising. Some methods include direct mail, email blasts, radio ads, Internet marketing, newspaper ads, public billboards, etc. Consider setting up a system to track what brings specific customers into your place of business. You need to know what form of advertising is working for you. The time-tested way to do this is by using tracking codes with your ad campaigns. Some businesses will offer a coupon or incentive with their advertising. For example, "You can save $5.00 with this coupon on any item purchased on our store until the end of July." When the customer brings in the coupon, the tracking code will identify which newspaper generated the lead. Some businesses ask the customer to say that "Mike from radio station XYZ sent me" to get the advertised special. Putting out various keywords for the same campaign can give you a tool to determine which methods worked better than others, and whether the return was effective enough to justify the cost of the ads.

Using a tracking system allows you to identify the advertising medium that brings the most customers into your place of business. Use all this information to better target your ideal customer. Obviously you don't want to spend advertising dollars if it is not generating customer leads.

The tracking system should not end there. You can get very specific even within the same advertising medium. By working with the ad sales department at a newspaper, for example, you can run different keywords on different days. For example, the Tuesday newspaper ad may have attracted 20 new customers, while the Sunday newspaper ad only attracted 10 new customers. Since you're paying more for the Sunday ad, perhaps it isn't worth the money for its effect on your sales. Over time, these numbers will gain significance. You need to know which advertising day resulted in the most sales (revenue dollars) for you.

When you begin to collect this data, you can then start to measure the return on your investment. It is obvious that you will not be continuing to advertise if no sales resulted for that particular form of advertising over a period of time (remember you are attempting to build a relationship with your ideal customer). However, looking at total revenue dollars generated is not the sole criteria. For example, if Tuesday's newspaper ad generated $4,000 and Sunday's ad generated $5,000 in sales, it does not mean that Sunday is the best day for you to run your newspaper ads. Let's introduce another element. Let's say it costs $1,000 to run an ad on Tuesdays and $2,500 to run Sunday's ad, when you analyze your rates of return you will see that Tuesday's ad resulted in a 300% rate of return, whereas the Sunday ad returned 100%.

11. When marketing, you need to understand the lifetime value of a customer. Which is the better customer? Spend $100 and obtain a customer who spends $150? Spend $1,000 to obtain a customer that spends $750? Don't be too hasty and say the first situation is the better customer because you made money with the first customer and lost money with the second customer. The correct answer is determined once all of the facts are known. If the first customer's lifetime spending for the business is $150, that customer's lifetime value is $50 net. If the second customer has an average life span of five years, then that customer's lifetime value is $2,750 net. Once all of the facts are known, the benefit of the second situation is easily seen as the better of the two.

12. Use the power of the Internet. A large number of your potential customers are trying to find solutions to their problems on the Internet. Get your business online. Hire a website developer to help you put together an online platform to get customers to your website and keep them engaged for more than a couple of seconds. The longer you can get a potential customer to stay on your Web page, the more chance you'll have to communicate your unique selling proposition or value proposition. Make sure it's easy for your potential customers to contact you. We recently read that the average

person spends only 10 seconds on a website's landing page. If they do not find what they are looking for (you solving their problem or needs) in those 10 seconds, they move on. Thus, it is important that your headline focus on the ideal customer's needs and how your business can provide the solution.

We often see business websites that focus on the business and not the needs of the ideal customer. Now that you recognize that the viewer of your website will determine in a matter of seconds whether to explore your website or move on, do you really want to put your company's history or your personal motivations for starting a small business at the top of the page? Why would your ideal customer care about that yet? For example, if your ideal customer is a male teenager looking for action video games, he likely does not care that you are a family-owned business that has been in the same location for 20 years. If he doesn't see what he came for in the 10-second time span, he will likely head right back to the search engine. Instead, your website would be better positioned by having a headline that reads "10 Most Popular Action-Packed Video Games of 2014" and having a short professionally produced video below the headline that the viewer can watch to learn more about how he can order those video games directly from your company.

To provide your website visitor with information about your company, rather than using an "About Us" page just like all other websites, consider an alternative format. Make use of testimonials from satisfied customers to help explain why they buy from you. The best part of owning a website is that you can change the format from time to time, so you may want to experiment.

13. When it comes down to brass tacks, marketing is all about sales. This is why you should know the difference between lead generation and lead conversion. Ads are often measured in terms of lead generations, but not all leads will end in a sale. The most important measure is lead conversion. While you must have lead generations to have lead conversions, it is most important to understand that regardless of how many lead generations you are getting, if you cannot convert those

lead generations to a sale, they are of little value and you must re-strategize your closing process. These facts are of particular interest for the small business that specializes in a service.

14. Offer a guarantee. The guarantee takes away some of the anxiety when a customer is working with someone new. The guarantee removes a potential barrier to obtaining that new ideal customer. Business owners are sometimes reluctant to offer a guarantee for fear that unscrupulous consumers will take advantage. While there may always be a few customers who will take advantage of a guarantee, on the other hand, such a guarantee may have provided assurance to dozens or hundreds of others who became good customers. You will quickly discern the ideal customers who are worth keeping versus those who should not receive your continued efforts. For example, we are one of the few CPA firms that offer a guarantee. What has it cost us? In terms of dollars, very little. Yes, we have had a couple of clients say that they were not totally satisfied and requested a fee adjustment. We view this as a positive relationship-building step. First, we immediately agree to adjust our fee even if we may have some hesitation regarding the merit of the claim. The important factor is that it has merit in the mind of our client. By quickly living up to our end of the bargain, we've satisfied the customer and shown that we care about meeting his expectations. Second, we listen carefully to why the client requested the adjustment. Perhaps our instructions or comments were not clearly understood by the client. If we can learn from this experience to better communicate with our clients, we can avoid these situations in the future and will be the better for it. By doing all this, we may find that the disgruntled customer will trust us enough to give us business again in the future. Of course, it is always our prerogative to determine whether we desire to continue as well.

15. Live by a marketing calendar. You will need to devote time to marketing either daily or weekly. You must make it a point to

keep these appointments with yourself. Remember also that in a larger sense, your marketing campaigns will drive your business, just like the moon's gravity moves the tides. Use your marketing calendar to help prepare for the waves and make sure that you aren't inundated before you're ready.

We had mentioned the importance of listening to experts in the field. We wish to share with you our experiences with two marketing firms.

Ian Brodie is a marketing consultant based in the United Kingdom whose marketing advice I enjoy reading. He has a great sense of humor and some very insightful tips. Ian is very open about what marketing techniques he has tried and how his programs have fared. When something doesn't work, he readily admits his "failure," makes the appropriate changes, and marches onward to convert them to future successes. If you subscribe to Ian's email newsletters, you will quickly learn that he practices being in constant contact with his prospects sharing his insights. Ian's web address is: www.ianbrodie.com.

Ian has published a list of five marketing tips regarding particularly damaging beliefs that one must recognize if one's business is to be successful.

Crippling Belief #1: "If I do good work, people will hear about me." Ian writes that this is a myth. Good news does not necessarily travel, and it never travels as energetically as bad news. According to his background research, when a person has a bad experience with a business, an average of about 12 people will hear about it, and those 12 people will each tell six others. If a person has a good experience, he'll share that with a couple of friends. Ian is also troubled with the "word of mouth" strategy because it is dependent upon your customer's action and is passive on your part. You are relying upon the goodwill of others to generate business for you. It's a matter of where you will focus your energy.

Crippling Belief #2: "I just need to get my name out there." Ian disagrees with this thought process as well. This myth makes people pay for advertising, send out meaningless flyers, and hire search engine optimization companies to generate traffic to dead-end websites. He recommends instead that you develop a unique selling proposition and a targeted strategy.

Crippling Belief #3: "I can copy what others are succeeding with." Ian says that the painful truth is that while a strategy may be working for one business, it is not guaranteed to work for you. There are too many small, unknown differences among situations—your ideal customer or your skills may be different. Ian recommends that you learn from others but find what works for you and then become a master of that.

Crippling Belief #4: "I can't find the time for marketing." I really enjoyed reading Ian's description of this myth, because we hear a very similar phrase all the time in our field of expertise: "I can't find the time for working on my financials." As Ian says, "You don't *find* the time for marketing—you *make* the time. If you don't market, you'll soon have plenty of time on your hands." Ian has noticed in his marketing consultations, as we have in our financial consultations, that people avoid marketing (or their financials) because they don't feel comfortable with tasks that they are not innately good at or that they don't enjoy doing. But don't let this stop you! Earlier in this book, I shared with you that I experienced this same mindset before realizing that if I were to spend the time and energy on marketing, I could become very good at it. You can do this too.

Crippling Belief #5: "I'm not a (natural) salesperson." Ian jokes that "natural salespeople" don't just pop out of their mother's womb. They learned to do it. When you look at people who are good at selling, you are looking at the finished product—the product of years of experience and training.

Another of our favorite small-business gurus is Kirk Ward. He is a retired Enrolled Agent and currently markets to accountants and consultants. Kirk's website address is http://instantpracticebuilder.com/home. We have had numerous telephone conversations with Kirk, and we find a lot of value in his hands-on-experience, plus his sense of humor is a real relief from the dryness of your typical consultant. Kirk says that there are four important questions that the business owner must ask himself:

1. **Why should customers do business with you?** The business owner needs to realize that there is nothing special about his business unless it has a unique selling proposition that is needed by the ideal target customer.

2. **How do you create excitement about your service or product?** Again if your product or service is like everyone else's, what appeal is there for the targeted ideal customer to do business with you? The customer needs to be receiving a perceived value by giving you money for your product or service.

3. **How do you make money?** We have touched upon this question by recommending that all potential business owners understand their ideal customer profiles and how to attract those customers. Included in this dictum is the requirement that you understand the financial metrics of your business, and your must have a step-by-step framework for how to increase cash flows.

4. **What are the values you live by?** Kirk suggests that every business develop its own working culture and values. These will give your business a sense of morals and precepts to live by, to share with future employees, and to communicate to customers as an integral part of your brand.

CHAPTER 18

How Do You Increase the Value of Your Business?

This question should be one of the business owner's primary focuses when starting the business as well as throughout the life of the business. If you do go into business for yourself, would you not want to maximize that value? You might think this question is always on a business owner's mind, but that is often not the case. Far too many small-business people attempt to wear too many hats. It's really difficult to take responsibility for marketing, financial affairs, workforce management, customer service, and a host of other daily activities of the company. There aren't enough hours in the day to tend to all of these responsibilities. Something's got to give, and that explains why many business owners fail to spend "the necessary time on the marketing and financial aspects" of their business.

There are many reasons why this "superman" small-business owner tries to do everything by himself:

- He is attempting to control his costs by not paying the premium for competent employees or consultants to manage certain aspects of his business;

- He may be a stubborn perfectionist who believes that nobody can do the job as good as he can;
- He believes since his family members are often assisting him that he is not doing everything himself;
- He doesn't appreciate the value that diversifying can bring to his business.

Unfortunately, some business owners only begin to think about the value of their business at the time they consider selling it. I would bet that these are also those owners who have resisted working with a team of trusted advisors throughout the life cycle of their business. The strategy of doing everything yourself will very likely substantially reduce the value of your business, and this will become painfully clear at the time you engage a business broker to help you sell the small business, or when you meet with a financial advisor to pin down the current financial health of your operation for a bridge loan. A potential buyer, when evaluating the business, will see from a generalized perspective and not from the eyes of its creator who has a hand in every daily task.

While it may be an absolute requirement for the owner to be involved in every task to get started according to the plan, it is important to wean yourself away from the daily operations at some point so that you can execute a larger strategy to increase value.

So what should the business owner be doing to increase the value of the business? As you read through this list, consider the sticking points that a potential buyer of your business would bring up. Your job as the owner and eventual seller is to remove reasons why the buyer would demand a lower sales price or hesitate to buy at all. To get the most value from what you've built, you want the buyer to be ecstatic and enthused about the opportunity to buy an established business. If there are areas of concern, then you may find that you've sold the business for much less than it could have been worth; or you may not be able to sell at all.

- **A business grows by increasing sales every year.** This is likely the most important factor to a potential buyer. Seeing annual sales increases each year gives the buyer confidence that the business has growth potential, and hence you can command a higher multiple of your revenues. The buyer will envision not only running this already successful business but also increasing sales by making changes. If sales are declining or sporadically increasing and decreasing from year to year for reasons that you can't explain, the buyer will be concerned that you've gotten this far only on luck or chance. It will be easy for that potential buyer to imagine there is an inherent problem with the business, and it's only still running because you, the original owner, burned the candle at both ends to keep it afloat. If sales did dip or change from year to year, you should document what happened and give a convincing explanation, show that you addressed it, and that sales have increased thereafter.

- **To create a self-sustaining business, you need to remove yourself.** Yes, you have worked long and hard hours to grow your business and make it a financial success. You are without any doubt the key to the success of your business. However, from the perspective of the buyer, you are replaceable. More importantly, in the eyes of the buyer you must be replaceable. The buyer is purchasing your business, not you. If you have continuously worn every hat in your business, what happens when you sell it and retire? What will be the reaction of the employees of the company once you are gone? Will the customers still do business with your company? Will vendors still wish to deal with the business on the same terms once you are removed from the business? Will the business fail because you are no longer there? Your buyer may doubt all these things if you have not built a workplace that can function without your direction every moment. These doubts could easily have been dispelled if you had key people working in the business for you. All of the previously mentioned concerns racing through the buyer's mind would be erased because the buyer realizes that the business will continuously operate as it has in the past even after your departure. Again, the buyer wants to purchase "a business" and not your services. The buyer needs to know that the business will be successful when you depart.

- **Diversify your customer base.** If a large percentage of your business is dependent upon one or a few key customers, this increases a buyer's risk when purchasing your business. What happens if one or more of those key customers moves on? Your cash flow projections used to value your business will go up in smoke. Your buyer would lose the ability to service the debt taken on to purchase your business, or would not be able to take a salary to pay his bills. A savvy buyer will recognize these weaknesses and offer you a purchase price that is heavily discounted to protect against these scenarios. The end result is that you've decreased the value of your business by depending on too narrow a customer base. While it is nice to have individual customers or single contracts that generate significant sales and cash flows for your business, it is imperative that you have a large, diversified pool of customers so that the company's success is not dependent upon one or a few key customers. As a rule of thumb, no one single customer should constitute more than 20% of your sales.

- **Develop your company's most important assets—the employees.** If you have a strong employee base and a great management team, your potential buyer has the comfort of knowing that a change in ownership would have little impact on the company's most valuable asset. While your financials and cash flows will be a major factor in the value of your company, your most valuable asset is not reflected on those financials. The financials and cash flow are the starting point to determine the value of your business. The valuation report will then consider other factors that can either increase or decrease that preliminary valuation. The strength of your most valuable asset, your employees, can substantially increase your company's overall value.

- **Remove family members as employees.** While your family members may be doing an excellent job, their presence will wave a red flag to the buyer. Are family members being overpaid compared to non-family members? Will family members have the same allegiance and dedication to the buyer as they had to the seller? Will family members leave the business after the change of ownership because the family atmosphere has been lost? Would they create an atmosphere of resentment or defiance to any changes? To increase the value of your business, you need to strengthen your company's most valuable asset, its employees, and replace family members. Again, by doing this you are removing a reason for the buyer not to offer full value for your business.

- **Make sure your financial statements reflect the true results of your business.** The cash flow of your business is sometimes referred to as EBITDA. This means <u>e</u>arnings <u>b</u>efore <u>i</u>ncome <u>t</u>axes, <u>d</u>epreciation and <u>a</u>mortization. Your business's historical and current EBITA will also forecast the cash flows that the new business owner will depend upon. Occasionally, when working with a client who was interested in purchasing a business, we would hear the business owner's assurance that "the actual cash flows are better than the financials reflect." This was supposedly true because the business owner had not reported cash sales and would also pay for his personal expenses using business accounts. By sharing this information with the prospective buyer, has this seller enhanced the value of his business? What has this seller actually done? He has admitted to the prospective buyer that he habitually commits tax fraud, and is in general morally flexible when it comes to his finances. If the business owner was not afraid of falsifying his tax returns (lying to the IRS), how can any representations he makes about the business to you be relied upon? We purposely referred to the buyer as the "prospective buyer," because what the seller has done is to ensure that a savvy prospective buyer will continue prospecting to find another business to purchase.

- **Start the process of "selling" your business as early as possible**. Most business owners do not wake up one morning and say "I am going to sell my business today." They start to think about it much earlier than that. In the years before they decide to sell, they ask themselves questions. Do they want to continue the business? Do they want to start another type of business? When would they like to retire? Will their health allow them to continue in the business? When these thoughts begin, it is time to *plan* for the sale of your business. Planning to sell does not necessarily mean that you will sell the business. It may be just a contingency plan. However, once you begin to think about it and discuss the option with your team of trusted advisors, you will definitely consider the long-term steps that you need to take to increase the value of your business. At this stage, a business valuation expert can be added to your team of advisors. Looking at the items discussed above, it is reasonable to say that all of those steps cannot be implemented overnight. Rather, those steps may take a couple of years to implement, which is why it is so important to start the planning process as early as possible.

Part Four

Exit Strategy

CHAPTER 19

Do You Have An Exit Strategy?

U p to this point in the book we have addressed points about starting and growing your business. A good business plan should also have a plan to get out . . . your exit strategy. Will you be selling the business? Do you plan to leave the business to one child or to all of your children? You will have invested so much of your energy, money, and time growing the business. Do you have a plan to take some or all of that equity back out of the business? The committed entrepreneur needs to give the exit strategy serious consideration. Given how challenging it is to start a business and keep it running, the exit strategy is often completely ignored. Perhaps it's assumed that they will address it at a later date. But that later date can come unexpectedly soon in some cases. If you or someone in your family suffers a life-changing event before your exit plan is completed, the unexpected consequences can have a disastrous impact on the business and your personal life. Let's look at some of the methods used by entrepreneurs to plan for this kind of problem.

A Buy/Sell Agreement (BSA) is how most business owners memorialize their exit strategy. The BSA can be a standalone agreement, or it might be incorporated into another legal document, such as the company's bylaws or operating agreement. We personally prefer that the BSA be a separate agreement. Reviewing legal documents can be costly and time consuming. By keeping the BSA separate from an operating agreement, any change(s) to the BSA or the operating requirement do not require your lawyer to review pages related to both legal documents.

A BSA provides some certainty in an uncertain world. If you have gone into business with a partner, there may come a day when you can no longer work together or one partner passes away. A BSA prescribes the rights and obligations of the owners and provides a framework for how the ownership interests will pass between the parties. It defines how the business will be valued should one partner wish to purchase the ownership interest of another partner. Without a BSA, any change in ownership can lead to a legal impasse, long and expensive litigation, and a lack of leverage when negotiating the transfer of the ownership interest. These events will often result in a diminishment of the business enterprise value.

New business owners often skirt this issue, saying that a BSA is not needed because the partners are the best of friends. Just like a prenuptial agreement, the discussion of a BSA might be considered taboo, or an abridgment of trust between the partners. When we hear this argument, we remind our clients of the fact that roughly 50% of all marriages in this country wind up in divorce court. Those partners were on the very best of terms when they were legally bound together as well. All too often, our counsel falls on deaf ears, but we can only advise again that a new business owner should prepare for all contingencies, even a worst-case scenario.

It's a fact that CPAs and attorneys see business owner conflicts happen more often than most entrepreneurs. We've seen that worst-case scenario, which is why we continue to advise the new business owner that a BSA is a must from the very earliest stages of the business. Far too many owners figure they'll negotiate the BSA at a later date. Would you like to guess when that later date usually occurs? Yes, that's correct— the date they realize a BSA is needed is after some triggering event has occurred. Since there is no agreement in place, there are no terms for an orderly transition, and perhaps there are no insurance monies available to the surviving partner to buy out the ownership interest of the deceased partner. Unfortunately for the business owner who takes this approach, he is jeopardizing the future of his company and his family at a very critical time.

Triggering Events are events that can cause the BSA to become immediately effective. While the death of one partner is often the major event that a BSA agreement seeks to protect against, other triggering events include permanent disability of a partner, retirement, resignation, divorce, bankruptcy, felony charge, loss of a professional license to practice, ethical or regulatory disciplinary actions, attainment of a financial goal regarding the success of the business, disputes between the partners, and anything else that the business owners and their trusted team of advisors deem appropriate.

Permitted and Non-Permitted Transfers need to be identified. When drawing up a BSA, the current owners may have certain ownership situations they desire to avoid. Maybe they don't want the business to fall into the wrong hands, or they believe that the business should always have a certain leadership structure. If a potential interest of ownership transfer results in the business entity violating the number of owners allowed or the type of owners allowed by an S Corporation, the BSA needs to explicitly prevent these types of transfers.

What happens if one partner dies prematurely and the surviving spouse wants to step in as the new partner? Perhaps the surviving partner does not wish to be in business with the spouse. BSAs can include provisions that allow the surviving partner to purchase that share of the business from the spouse.

Providing a Guaranteed Market for the Transfer of the Ownership Interest at Fair Market Value is a provision that needs to be included in every BSA. The agreement needs to have a provision for a method of determining valuation so that the transfer is fair. Ideally, the "selling partner" receives fair value for that share of the business and the "purchasing partner" does not overpay. The BSA needs to address how that valuation will be calculated. Almost all small businesses do not have shares of financial interest that are readily tradable, which means there is not a market readily available to determine the value of the business.

Common valuation methods include:

- The partners mutually agree to an annual value for the business.
- Relying upon an industry norm or customizing the company valuation formula based on comparison of its metrics to similar businesses. For example, based on my experience working with the cable TV industry, a valuation rule-of-thumb is based on the industry's "average subscriber." The value for that single subscriber is multiplied by the number of cable subscribers for the cable franchise being purchased, giving a starting point for negotiating the value of the acquisition.
- The fair market valuation is usually determined by commissioning an appraisal or valuation study. This technique uses one or more third-party appraisers to independently value the business using professional valuation approaches. These are often primarily focused on the cash flows generated by the business. Looking at the historical and current results of the business determines a fair market value (usually a multiple of those revenues) that a willing buyer would pay to obtain those cash flows.
- The value of insurance proceeds is the value assigned to the value of the partner's interest. This approach has an inherent flaw, because a company's valuations are always changing. Business owners usually do not look at their insurance coverage after the insurance policy is purchased. Thus, while the true value of the business may be increasing, the life insurance value won't necessarily keep pace.
- Valuations are sometimes determined by combinations of multiple valuation methods. If a company uses a combination of valuation methods, often the BSA will include language that the business value cannot be "greater than" or "less than" the valuation methods used, or an average of such valuations.

We personally prefer a valuation method that uses an independent appraiser to perform a valuation study, especially if the study is needed as a result of a triggering event. While there will be a cost to have a valuation study done, the cost is generally not more than a few thousand dollars. Depending upon the circumstances of the triggering event, that cost may be worth every penny to avoid litigation by a dissatisfied party. A valuation study, when performed by an independent, third party provider, is based on the company's historical and projected cash flows and other market and economic factors. The criteria used by a professional valuation expert will usually be honored by the courts, whereas formulas or ratios arbitrarily demanded by business owners run a greater risk of not representing fair value by the courts. If the triggering event is caused by some personal tragedy, such as death or disability, it can be a very emotional time for all parties involved. Employing an independent party to determine the enterprise value should provide some comfort that the transferred ownership interest is equitable and fair. In addition to requiring a valuation study as a result of a triggering event, we believe that every company should have a periodic valuation study done. If an annual study is deemed unnecessary by the business, then consider doing one every three or five years. A history of valuation studies before the triggering event, when all parties were at full capacity, implies that the owners agreed about the true value of the business. This will give credence to any study done as a result of the triggering event.

We recently had a father and son start their business. The business plan stipulated that the cash flows from the business, which were not needed to expand the business operations, would be immediately withdrawn by the two partners. The two partners were investing sweat equity into the business. They would work long hours and generate revenues as a result of their efforts. The capital invested in the business would be minimal in comparison to revenues. By way of example, if the company generated $1 million in revenues and that money was distributed to the two partners, the company's bank account would be zero. The attorney drafting the company's BSA inserted language stipulating that the agreed value of the transfer between the two partners upon a triggering event would be equal to 50% of the company's book value. When we saw this provision in the draft BSA, we notified our clients that since they were withdrawing all cash from the business, which was the only tangible asset of the business, using book value as the transfer price would result in a transfer price of zero. Although the business would have significant intangible value, spouses of any deceased owner would receive nothing because of the language in the BSA. The attorney responded that since there was no book value at the date of the triggering event, the parties would need to agree to some other means to determine fair value at that time. We asked our client "What would be the result if the parties could not agree?" Would they really want to place this burden upon their spouses at such an emotional time? Fortunately, our clients decided that it would not be prudent to use net book value and had the attorney revise the transfer price language in the BSA to be determined by a valuation study done by an independent third party.

The purchase price is not necessarily always equal to the fair market value. For example, if the BSA's triggering event is the fact that a partner was convicted of a felony or had declared personal bankruptcy, it could be argued that those events reflect poorly on the business, possibly decreasing its value. Should the partner be paid the fair market value or a discounted value because of actions that have negatively impacted the business? Likewise, under circumstance described here, should the departing partner be paid immediately, or over some stipulated time period? One must not forget that such negative acts by one partner will place the remaining partner(s) under a financial hardship that may very well require that the business incur debt to meet its cash needs, or on a worst-case basis, be sold. A well-written BSA should consider such factors.

Tax planning is an excellent reason the CPA needs to be involved with the BSA. The BSA can be structured as a "stock redemption," in which the company buys back the interests; or the BSA can allow a "cross-purchase," in which the other owners or successors buy the interests directly. For tax planning purposes, the cross-purchase method gives the purchaser a "step-up" in basis on the received ownership interests. This means that the tax basis in the purchased interest is equal to what the successor owner had to pay to acquire that interest. With a stock redemption, the company makes the purchase rather than the remaining owner(s). This means that while the remaining owner(s) have an increase in the value of their respective interests, they do not get an increase in tax basis, since they did not purchase the stock from the exiting partner. In other words, their ownership interest was increased but they themselves did not pay anything. The tax basis issue does not come into play immediately, but will be relevant in the future if the remaining partner disposes or transfers his interest. The tax gain on a transfer or disposition is determined by the difference between the sales proceeds and the tax basis. Thus, a partner using the cross-purchase agreement would pay less in income taxes than the partner who obtained his additional ownership interest using a stock redemption.

On the other hand, although a partner in the stock redemption scenario would pay more in taxes for his increased interest, he did not have to lay out cash to fund that acquisition, since the company paid for it.

Rather than having either a redemption or cross-purchase agreement in the BSA, suggest giving the remaining owners the choice as to how the purchase should be made. Giving the remaining owners this option allows them to not only consider the tax consequences of the transfer, but also how the purchase will be funded. If the business has the funds to make the purchase and the remaining owner does not have the funds, it may be more convenient for all parties to have the company redeem (purchase) the shares of the departing partner.

Funding of the BSA is very important. To avoid concerns with non-liquidity and non-payment after a triggering event, life insurance is the tool most commonly used to fund BSA agreements. Life insurance can be held by the company, the other partners, successors of the deceased, or a separate trust. If the company receives the insurance proceeds, a stock redemption is often used to buy out the deceased owner's interest. If the other partners receive the life insurance proceeds, they now have the funding for a cross-purchase agreement.

A Forced Buy-Out Clause is sometimes included in a BSA, which allows one partner to force the sale of the business between the partners. An example of this would be where one partner (let's refer to him as Partner #1) makes a written offer to buy out another partner (let's refer to him as Partner #2). Upon receipt of Partner #1's offer, Partner #2 then has the option during a stipulated time period to accept Partner #1's offer or to buy out Partner #1 for the same exact terms of his offer. This type of arrangement places an enormous amount of pressure on Partner #1 to make a fair and reasonable offer as he realizes that Partner #2 has the right to purchase his ownership interest for that same value.

CHAPTER 20

Summary

We have discussed in this book two basic ways to start your own business.

The first is the path of least resistance. The soon-to-be business owner dives in head-first and focuses on opening the business as soon as possible. He thinks of it like he is a performance racecar driver whose strategy for a 12-hour race is to be the first driver to push the gas pedal. It's a shortsighted strategy, is it not? The usual scenario is that this person does all or many of the steps himself to get the business up and running. Rather than moving in an orderly and organized fashion, perhaps the steps that are perceived to be the easiest are completed first. These "easy" steps may include creating a legal entity and obtaining an EIN from the IRS. The business owner may attempt to create his own legal entity working directly with the Department of State or simply call an Internet service provider to create the legal entity for $200. He calls the IRS for an EIN or uses the IRS website to obtain the EIN. If there are 10 items on the to-do list he has created, he can immediately cross off two of them. Now he is thinking he's 20% done and has kept his start-up costs to $200. Next, he runs to the bank and opens a business checking account. Another step completed, and now he is 30% down his list. This rationalization continues until every item on the checklist is completed and he crosses the finish line.

If the business owner does consult with someone who suggests a different approach than that which the owner is following, those suggestions are sometimes quickly dismissed because they sound like too much work. Or they're dismissed for the simple reason that they deviate from the path the business owner desires to travel. The owner, without any prior business experience, is consciously or unconsciously looking for confirmation of his approach rather than advice as to how to do it correctly.

The costs incurred to start the new business are often paid from a personal checking account and are not properly accounted for, resulting in books and records of the new business that do not properly reflect the results of the new venture. In addition, possible tax deductions are overlooked, resulting in unnecessary tax obligations. Unfortunately, the business owner is totally unaware that the first two steps he completed affected his legal liability and how much he pays in taxes. While he only paid $200 and feels that he saved a couple of thousands of dollars in professional fees, he may learn the hard way that those two steps will cost him many thousands or tens of thousands of dollars over the next few years in additional taxes paid. Let's hope that he is never sued, because then he may find that the legal entity he created using an online program does not adequately protect his business and his family's assets.

Is it no wonder that statistics show that greater than 50 per cent of new businesses fail within the first five years? Some of these failed businesses were cases where the business owner and his family invested significant amounts of money. From our vantage point as tax advisors, we have seen this approach result in families losing their retirement funds or their personal residences to foreclosure. We've seen business owners who were regretful, ashamed, and embarrassed to tell their family and friends that the business wasn't working out and a bankruptcy filing was the only option. The most common reason for business failures such as these is that they were under-capitalized. While difficult to prove for lack of data at this point, we believe that a large percentage of small businesses that fail due to under-capitalization problems do so because their owners start their own business without preparing a business plan or gathering a team of trusted advisors to provide guidance and advice.

The second approach to starting your own business is to develop a well thought-out business plan based on many hours of due diligence on your part, and then to review those results with your trusted team of advisors. Is this a more costly approach? We admit that yes, it is without any doubt more expensive, at least initially. However, over the long run it will likely prove to be the least costly approach. Taking your time to do the job right will result in better legal liability protection, a tax structure that saves you money and headache, and an increased chance of success, which may result a nice rate of return on the money invested, rather than worry and fear about defaulting on bank loans or inability to repay family members who helped finance the business. This path also provides peace of mind, which is a priceless return on one's investment.

We hope that the readers of this book will find its guidance invaluable during the process of starting their own businesses. We want every one of you to become successful business owners. Re-read this book again in the future, and don't forget to highlight those sections of the book that you felt the need to address. Good luck to you as you develop your roadmap to financial success as a business owner. The road is long and it can be difficult to navigate, but we know you can reach your goals, because we've seen many others do it. We really love our jobs advising small-business owners, and we hope our advice has helped you in your own business.

APPENDIX A

Types Of Insurance Policies

Workers compensation insurance will be needed if you have employees. We personally like our clients to obtain this coverage from a private insurance company rather than from a state fund. The reason for this preference is that we believe that a private insurance company will act more as an advocate for the business owner because the insurance company has a vested interest in paying the insurance benefit only in those cases where the claim is valid. Our experience with state policies is that the state is less of an advocate for the business owner and is more of a claims processor. As a business owner, depending upon state law, you may be able to exclude yourself from state coverage should you desire to do so.

Professional liability or Errors and Omission (E&O) insurance is needed if you are going to provide professional services. While everyone may strive for perfection, few if any are able to achieve that objective, especially in the minds of the client, patient, or customer. If the professional makes an error, is negligent, or is found to have committed an act of malpractice, an E&O policy may provide coverage for the claim and in some cases the legal expenses incurred with respect to the claim.

General liability insurance is purchased to cover payments relating to claims for bodily injury, property damage, medical expenses, libel, slander, and the cost of defending lawsuits.

Product liability insurance is needed for those companies that manufacture, sell wholesale, distribute, or sell at retail a product that is found to have a safety defect. This is an area where an experienced insurance agent can be of immense value in determining the amount of coverage needed for your industry or product.

Commercial property insurance policies protect against losses related to damage from fire, smoke, storms, civil disobedience and acts of vandalism.

Home-based business insurance is often ignored by the small business owner. When meeting with small business owners who meet with clients and vendors using their home as their office, it is surprising how many of those business owners failed to communicate this fact with their insurance agent. The misstep of not notifying your insurance agent of your home office use, and not purchasing the needed riders to the homeowner's policy, could result in your business not being insured if the claim results from the commercial use of your personal residence. Keep in mind that these riders do have limits, and the business owner may need to purchase other types of insurance. This is another reason why working with an experienced small business insurance agent is so important.

Other "housekeeping" chores are necessary for business owners who work out of the home. If you belong to a homeowner's association (HOA), do the by-laws of the HOA permit you to operate a business out of your personal residence? You also need to check with the local zoning board to see if you can run a business from your home. Another consideration may be that even if you are legally allowed to run a business from your home, how will your neighbors react to you doing so?

Cyber-security insurance is relatively new. As a business owner, you may have access to sensitive and confidential information of your clients, customers, patients, and employees. A simple example is the credit card account information that your business processes. As I am writing this book, the Target department store chain has received a whole lot of adverse publicity about a security breach of the confidential information in its systems gained from hackers who breached their wireless networks, "targeting" customers who swiped their credit cards in the stores. The Target breach and others like it illustrate that sensitive information needs to be secured in your systems. It can extend to the internal files maintained on your server and also to your company's website. You want the information you gather from others to be readily available to you, and yet it needs to be secure to prevent your customers, employees and vendors from being put at risk.

Some of the other more common threats business owners face are website tampering, theft of data from by disgruntled employees or hackers, infections by malicious code, spyware and viruses that corrupt files to make them inaccurate or not readily available, identity theft, and phishing emails to trick you in giving out sensitive information.

Keep in mind that while there is a cost to purchase insurance coverage for cyber-security protection, that cost is likely very minimal when compared to the cost of rectifying a security breach.

APPENDIX B

An Example Of How To Compute The Debt Service Coverage Ratio

Assume that the business's net income + depreciation + amortization + interest expense − taxes = $75,000. The owner's net personal cash flow of salary + other personal income sources (e.g., interest and dividends) − household expenses − taxes = $67,000. The combined cash flow is equal to $142,000. Assume that the existing business debt that will not be retired or refinanced + the new debt requested equal $68,000. The personal debt service of the owner consists of a mortgage payment, an auto loan, and credit card debt equal to $24,000. The combined debt service obligations are equal to $92,000.

If the lender were to look solely at the business DSCR, a ratio of 1.1X is computed ($75,000 divided by $68,000). This ratio is less than the desired 1.2X.

Business Cash Flow   = $ 75,000
Business Debt   = $ 68,000
DSCR   = 1.1

However, if the global (combined) ratio is computed by including the personal cash flows, a global DSCR of 1.5X is computed ($142,000 divided by $92,000). Thus at least in this example, although the business failed to have a DSCR of at least 1.2X, by the lender using the global approach with a DSCR of 1.5X the business owner passes this "C" test.

Combined Cash Flows   = $142,000
Combined Debt   = $ 92,000
Combined DSCR   = 1.5

A Primer On SBA Loans

The most common SBA loan today is the 7(a) Loan Program. These 7(a) loans are used to establish a new business or to assist in the acquisition, operation, or expansion of an existing business. It is our understanding that the SBA is in the process of changing its standard operating procedures and will establish loan criteria for loans less than $350,000 and those greater or equal to $350,000. Thus, rather than focusing on a specific SBA loan program, let's review the SBA's overall lending program and how to apply for an SBA loan.

To obtain an SBA loan, the business owner works directly with an SBA-approved lender to negotiate the terms of the loan with that lender. As stated earlier, lenders find SBA loans attractive for those borrowers who may not meet the lender's ideal borrower credit profile because the federal government is guaranteeing that a large portion of the loan will be repaid to the bank should the borrower default. When SBA loans are involved, the lender has less personal discretion regarding the terms of the loan and information required to be submitted by the borrower because the federal government's rules and regulations must be followed.

There are three types of SBA loan lenders.

- The **Certified Lending Partners** program is being phased out, and thus we need not comment any further.

- A **General SBA lender** verifies the borrower's credit worthiness and the SBA does the same before the loan is approved. It usually takes two to three weeks to process the loan application.
- A **Preferred Lender Partner (PLP)** can have the loan approved within 24–48 hours. When dealing with a PLP, it is our understanding that the SBA does not verify the creditworthiness of every borrower when the loan application is being processed, but rather does so on a spot-check basis. The SBA is heavily relying upon the credit due diligence of the PLP lender. In other words, if the PLP approves the loan, the SBA automatically approves the loan in most cases. In addition to spot-checking PLP loan applications, the SBA also conducts periodic reviews of PLP loan application procedures, and the SBA will also review the PLP's due diligence on the credit if the borrower defaults on the loan.

For loans of $150,000 or more, the SBA guarantees 75% of the loan. For loans of less than $150,000, the SBA guarantees 85% of the loan. The SBA also has an SBA Express program where the loan application will be addressed within 36 hours. The SBA guarantees 50% of Express Loans.

As stated earlier, if the borrower has less than stellar credit, the lender will likely place the loan through the SBA's loan program. On the other hand, if the business owner has a very strong 5 C credit worthiness, the lender may be inclined to make the loan without going through the SBA program. In such cases, the lender believes that the borrowers' credit is so good that it would rather place the loan itself than pay the SBA's fees to place the loan through the SBA program.

The SBA does charge the lender a fee for guaranteeing the loan. This fee is based on the loan's maturity (the length of the loan) and the dollar amount guaranteed by the SBA, not the total amount of the loan. This fee is initially paid by the lender and passed on to the borrower either at closing or is included in the loan balance and is paid over the term of the loan.

In addition, the SBA charges the lender a monthly fee. While the lender cannot pass this fee on to the borrower, this cost would be reflected in the interest rate that the lender is charging the borrower.

The SBA pegs its interest rate to one of three acceptable base rates, which are the prime rate published by the *Wall Street Journal*, the LIBOR (London Interbank One prime Rate), and an SBA Peg Rate. The lender is allowed to add an additional spread to the base rate to arrive at the final interest rate. For loans with maturities of less than 7 years, the maximum spread cannot be greater than 2.25%. For loans with maturities of 7 years or longer, the maximum spread cannot exceed 2.75%. The spread on loans under $50,000 and those loans processed through the Express Loan program, the spreads can be greater.

Thus, if the borrower were to compare the cost of an SBA loan at different lenders, the cost of the loan would likely vary, as each lender is setting its own terms within the guidelines allowed by the SBA and its evaluation of the creditworthiness of the borrower.

While the SBA does not *require* collateral for every one of its loan programs, if collateral is available, be assured that the SBA will require that the lender securitize the loan to the extent of the collateral available.

An often-overlooked fact is that SBA loans are not required to have a variable (or floating) rate—they can have a fixed rate. Since many lenders will resell the guaranteed portion of an SBA loan to private investors, a more attractive premium can be earned by the lender with a variable rate. The variable rate protects the investor's return in case interest rates rise. Since today's (2009–2014) interest rates are historically speaking very low, investors would likely shy away from a fixed rate loan. When dealing with the SBA lender, you as the borrower should inquire if the loan will be resold or maintained as part of the lender's loan portfolio. In the latter case, you may be able to negotiate for a fixed rate of interest to protect against any rise in rates.

While SBA loans are not allowed to have balloon payments, the loans can be structured at a fixed rate for a period certain and then move to a variable rate. The borrower may also be able to negotiate for an interest-only loan during the early years of the loan to allow the business to generate better cash flows before it makes the full monthly payment.

Most SBA loans are repaid with monthly payments of principal and interest. If a fixed interest rate loan has been negotiated, the monthly payment to the bank will be the same each month. If the loan was a variable interest rate loan, the monthly payment will fluctuate as the interest rate changes. Similar to a mortgage payment on the purchase of a primary residence, a portion of each payment is interest (the cost of borrowing) and the remaining portion is principal (the repayment of the loan). Generally when looking at a loan amortization schedule (for loan periods of greater than 10 years), interest will comprise the majority of each payment, and only a small portion of your payment is allocated to the loan's principal. If a fixed interest rate loan was negotiated, each payment will decrease the amount of interest paid, and the amount allocated to debt repayment (principal) increases. This would not necessarily be true if a variable rate loan was used.

As a quick recap, you can reduce the monthly debt service cost and increase your cash flows by either negotiating a lower interest rate with the lender or by signing an interest-only loan, or a low fixed rate for a fixed period before the variable rate takes effect.

With debt, outgoing cash flows can also be reduced if the loan amortization period is extended. A SBA loan affords the business owner with attractive amortization periods. Whereas the typical lender would expect a loan for the acquisition of machinery and equipment to be repaid within 5–7 years, the SBA has a 10-year amortization period. For working capital needs, lenders typically expect the loan to be repaid within 1–3 years. The SBA has 7–10 year amortization periods. Inventory is typically three years borrowing directly from a lender, versus 10 years for an SBA loan. So when deciding whether to borrow directly from a lender who may be able to offer a lower interest rate because the lender is not incurring SBA fees, the business may find the SBA loan more attractive because of its longer amortization periods.

When requesting a loan, it is very important that the borrower have a rock solid business plan that adequately projects the business's cash flow needs. When working with our clients, we always recommend that the business owner do a cash flow projection on a "worst-case" basis. A "worst-case" scenario reflects what happens if the projected revenues are not met or an unexpected expenditure surfaces. Doing the financial cash flows of a business plan using an Excel worksheet allows the business owner to make modifications to the cash flow model. The borrower is better off requesting a loan for the cash indicated per the "worst-case" scenario rather than borrowing based on the "expected" business plan projection. Think of this as a contingency plan. If the worst happens, the business will have sufficient cash to meet those unexpected developments.

An SBA loan is considered to be in default if there are 60 days of non-payment. If there is a default on an SBA loan, the borrower cannot obtain any type of federal financing (e.g., student loan or FHA loan), all IRS income tax refunds will be automatically used to repay the federal government for its guaranteed repayment to the lender, the borrower may lose a portion of his monthly social security benefits as a partial repayment to the federal government, and the borrower's wages can be garnished.

The SBA has an Offer-In-Compromise (OIC) program, which is handled by the U.S. Treasury Department. The OIC program reviews the financial situation of the borrower, and if the borrower qualifies under the OIC program, the borrower may be able to settle the debt with the SBA for less than the full amount with a single lump-sum program (minimum payment of 20% of the balance due) or enter into a five-year monthly installment arrangement to settle the debt. The acceptance of an OIC will release the borrower from having to repay the full amount of the loan and he will not have his social security benefits reduced and his wages garnished. Even if the OIC is accepted, the borrower will not be able to obtain federal financing and will not be entitled to receive any IRS income tax refunds until the difference between the amount of the guaranteed loan amount and the amount paid via the OIC program is repaid.

APPENDIX D

A Primer On Loans That Are Not Repaid

If there was no intent to repay the monies advanced when the monies were transferred, then in the eyes of the IRS the parties did not make a loan. If the parties want the cash transfer to be treated as a loan, it needs to have all of the elements of a loan, which include a loan agreement, collateral, a fair interest rate, and a loan repayment period. If a required payment is not made, then collection efforts need to be made to demonstrate that the advance of funds was indeed a loan.

Assuming that a loan was made, the IRS recognizes two types of loans: business and non-business (personal) loans. It is important to realize that there are different tax treatments for business and personal loans. Generally, a business bad debt is one that comes from operating your trade or business. A business can incur bad debt from many sources, including credit extended to a customer or supplier, credit sales to customers, and through business loan guarantees. A business deducts its bad debts from its gross income when figuring its taxable income. Business bad debts may be deducted in part or in full depending upon the facts and circumstances. You can claim a business bad debt using either the specific charge-off method or the nonaccrual-experience method.

In a case where the business owner, a friend or relative is advancing funds to the business, the fact that the loan is being made to a business does not make it a business loan. These types of loans are considered personal loans by the IRS. Personal loans that have become uncollectible must be totally worthless to be tax deductible. You cannot deduct a partially worthless personal bad debt as a tax deduction.

A debt becomes worthless when the surrounding facts and circumstances indicate there is no reasonable expectation of payment. To show that a debt is worthless, the lender must establish that he has taken reasonable steps to collect the debt. It is not necessary to go to court if you can show that a judgment from the court would be uncollectible. You may take the deduction only in the year the debt becomes worthless. You do not have to wait until a debt is due to determine whether it is worthless.

A common issue with personal loans is that while these loans are theoretically no different than borrowing from a bank, they often become troublesome because of lack of documentation. When dealing with a bank or other institutional lender, the loan is legally documented with a loan agreement and is treated by both the borrower and lender as a loan. If the personal loan is repaid according to the terms of the loan agreement between the parties, these loans do not usually pose any problem with respect to the IRS. However, these loans become troublesome when the loan is in default (the required loan payments have not been made as per the loan agreement). The lender now finds that he is in the position of having lent money to a business and is uncertain that he will be repaid. The lender will now inform his tax professional to write off the loan as a bad debt on the lender's tax return. The lender is thinking that a tax deduction is better than nothing.

A personal bad debt is reported as a short-term capital loss on IRS Form 8949, *Sales and Other Dispositions of Capital Assets,* and also on IRS Form Schedule D. Depending upon other transactions that may be reported on Schedule D, the lender may be limited to an annual $3,000 reportable loss. If $30,000 was lent, it could possibly take the lender 10 years to write off that loss. A personal bad debt deduction requires a separate detailed statement attached to your return, which can increase the odds of being audited by the IRS. Since the IRS not only imposes penalties on taxpayers but also on tax preparers for taking deductions for which there is no supportable position, a good tax professional will carefully scrutinize the taxpayer's documentation for claiming a bad debt, so that he too can avoid the imposition of penalties on the client and the preparer.

The preparer realizes that when dealing with the IRS, if you want the loan treated as a loan, it is important that you have a loan agreement and that the terms of the loan agreement be followed. First, was it treated as an arm's-length loan between the two parties? One test is whether an arm's-length interest rate was charged between the parties. The IRS publishes each month its adjusted applicable federal interest rates (AFR). The lender must have charged at least the minimum AFR as published by the IRS in the month that the loan note was executed.

Think of the differences between borrowing from an institutional lender and a relative. While there may possibly exist a written loan agreement (verbal agreements are acceptable but harder to document for IRS tax purposes), often the principal parties of the personal loan agreement have not adhered to the terms of the loan agreement. For example, when a scheduled loan payment is missed, the bank will contact the borrower and demand payment. If sufficient payments are missed (60 days for SBA loans), the bank will notify the borrower that the loan is in default and perhaps foreclose on the loan. The bank will take steps to recover their loan by liquidating the collateral on the loan. When personal loans are in default, usually no immediate action is taken by the lender because of the personal relationship with the borrower. Aside from a possible telephone conversation or two between the parties about the status of the loan repayment, there is no written documentation or evidence between the parties demonstrating that the lender requested the repayment of the loan. The personal friend or relative may be reluctant to take legal action to foreclose on the loan.

The tax professional is faced with a multitude of issues. The owner of the business who lent money to his business may believe that he has a business loan bad debt that can be deducted against other sources of income, such as W-2 compensation. The CPA will need to educate the client why the loan is a personal loan, that the owner has a capital loss and not an ordinary loss that can be used to offset other sources of income, and that personal bad debts are limited to an annual maximum $3,000 capital loss deduction. Assuming the transfer of funds was a loan, a determination will need to be made as to when it did become worthless. The fact that the lender is now requesting a tax deduction does not in itself make the loan worthless. The loan became worthless when the loan went into default and collection efforts by the lender were not productive. If it is determined that the loan became worthless in an earlier year, then the claimant would need to submit an amended tax return if the statute of limitations is still open for that year.

If the loan is between the owner of a business and his corporation, and the repayments to the owner by the business are not recognized by the IRS as a loan but as compensation paid to the owner, then the IRS will assess penalties for failure to timely remit payroll taxes dating back to the date when the supposed loan repayments were made.

If it is determined that the amount lent was not to have been treated as a loan, the parties may mutually agree that the funds were an equity investment in the business. Depending upon the type of tax entity, distributions from the equity of a corporation can have some unexpected and less than desirable tax consequences. For example, an S Corporation may find itself having made disproportionate distributions to its shareholders, which could jeopardize its S Corporation status. C Corporations may be found to have made distributions to its shareholders, which are taxed to them personally and are not tax deductible by the corporation.

APPENDIX E

A Primer On Rollovers As Business Start-Ups (ROBS)

Here is a brief overview as to how a typical ROBS works. When an individual lacks liquid funds to start or purchase a business, he may be asked by a franchisor or business broker about the amount of retirement funds he has. If the retirement funds are sufficient, the promoter explains to the business owner that normally when retirement accounts are used to fund a business, the amounts distributed to the owner are subject to federal income taxes. If the owner is not aged 59 ½ or older, then those distributions are also subject to a 10% penalty. The taxability of the distributions and the 10% penalty, if applicable, are sufficient deterrents to prevent most people from using these funds to finance the business. Then comes the critical question: "If I (the broker, franchisor or promoter) could show you a way to use your retirement funds to finance a business and pay no income taxes and not be subject to the 10% penalty, in other words, have the IRS fund the purchase of your business, would you be interested?" Who would not be? In addition, since the funds are considered equity capital rather than debt capital, the business's cash flows will increase, because there will be no bank debt to repay.

A typical ROBS transaction involves using the owner's self-directed IRA (Individual Retirement Account) to fund the business. Either the business owner has a pre-existing IRA or an existing 401(k) retirement fund. If it's the latter, the business owner rolls over the 401(k) fund to a self-directed IRA. The promoter of the ROBS assists the business owner to create a C Corporation (a topic discussed earlier in this book) for the owner. The corporation then adopts a 401(k) plan. The 401(k) plan includes a provision that allows the plan's participants (the business owner) to transfer funds from his IRAs to the company 401(k) plan. When the owner transfers his IRA funds to the 401(k) plan, the promoter then directs the 401(k) plan to purchase employer stock in the C Corporation. Once the C Corporation receives the funds from the sale of the company stock, it uses those funds to purchase a business, a franchise, machinery and equipment, inventory, whatever the business needs.

Up to this point, a ROBS transaction does sound very appealing. The entrepreneur can obtain financing for the acquisition of his business without having to deal with those lenders who require a business plan; in addition, the business owner needs not pay any interest since there is no debt; the IRS is providing a portion of the funding (by the avoidance of taxes); the promoter can accomplish all of this in a very short timeframe; the promoter's cost is approximately $5,000, which may be less than the lender's closing fees if a bank loan were obtained; and the owner's equity investment in his business will be funding his retirement plan. The promoter may even inform the owner that the IRS has issued private letter rulings acknowledging that these plans work. However, the professional who is promoting this method may not explain to the entrepreneur that the IRS does not allow other taxpayers to rely upon these private rulings.

Do these plans work? They sound almost too good to be true. While we will acknowledge that these plans may work under certain circumstances, they also come with many pitfalls, and unless the business owner is working very closely with a tax advisor and attorney, the consequences for failing to comply with the IRS and U.S. Department of Labor (DOL) rules can be devastating.

Does the person who promotes this financing method pull back the layers of the onion and share the downsides and risks of a ROBS with the potential business owner who is considering using retirement funds for a venture? Even if the business owner was advised that there are very significant regulatory compliance requirements with this method, the owner may not fully comprehend the costs and restraints of compliance—because the owner is delirious with delight that he avoided paying significant taxes to the IRS and did not have to bother with applying for a bank loan. What are those costs and restraints? When you are dealing with a qualified retirement plan, such as a 401(k), you must remain compliant with ERISA, the federal law governing qualified retirement plans. Retirement plans are governed by the IRS and the DOL. Both departments have investigated the implementation of the ROBS method and have publicly stated that they will pursue businesses that do not follow the full letter of the law. The IRS published a memorandum that declared that ROBS transactions "may violate law in several regards." In other words, the IRS will look at ROBS transactions on a case-by-case basis and determine whether your plan is ERISA compliant. For those who believe the IRS does not have a sense of humor, the assigning of the "ROBS" acronym to these transactions might show a humorous side to the IRS.

One of the major risks associated with these plans is that the business owner will use the company's funds for personal use. First, the business owner mistakenly believes that the business belongs to him. In fact, it does not! The company's 401(k) plan owns the business! Second, the business owner believes that since it was his money that capitalized the business, the funds in the corporation belong to him. They do not. The assets of the corporation, including its cash, are owned by the 401(k) plan, the owner of the corporation. In the eyes of the IRS, the C Corporation is a different taxpayer than the owner, and the assets of one taxpayer cannot be co-mingled with the assets of another taxpayer.

Once the business is operating, the business owner has forgotten about any "do nots" that the CPA, legal counsel, or promoter may have shared. If the owner is not closely working with an accountant and business attorney, they are not there to remind him of what he must do and what he cannot do. Remember that we discussed earlier that many business owners get so wrapped up with running the business that they ignore the finances. Here is a prime example as to why tending to the financial aspects of a business must be done on a frequent basis. ERISA contains prohibited transactions, one of which disallows self-dealing. In other words, if the owner receives a personal benefit, he has violated ERISA law. Complicating matters is that the business owner is likely not paying sufficient attention to the company's books and records (a topic of discussion earlier in this book), and is not properly recording business transactions. If the owner needs to buy groceries on the way home and uses the company credit card rather than his personal credit card, he has used company funds (owned by the 401(k) plan) for personal use. Likewise, if the business is starting off very slow and the owner needs funds to pay his mortgage or rent and takes monies from the corporation, it is a prohibited transaction. The company 401(k) plan is for the benefit of all employees, and when the owner receives a self-dealing benefit, the retirement plan has discriminated against the other employees (even if there are no other employees).

The penalty for self-dealing is very costly. If evidence of self-dealing is found, the IRS treats 100 percent of the funds contributed from the owner's IRA to the company 401(k) plan as a deemed distribution, meaning that the entire amount is considered a taxable distribution to the owner. If the owner is not older than 59 ½, the funds distributed are subject to the 10% early withdrawal penalty. Ouch! If that were not bad enough, it can get worse. Assume that the owner does not have the funds to pay the tax assessment due to the deemed distribution. After all, the ROBS funding technique was used because of a lack of funds when originally creating the company. If the owner decides to use the cash in the corporation to pay his personal income taxes, the cash that is distributed from the C Corporation will very likely be treated by the IRS as compensation subject to payroll taxes. Questions that immediately come to mind are (1) is the owner a shareholder or does the 401(k) plan hold 100% of the outstanding shares? If the owner holds no stock in his company, he cannot argue that the monies paid to him are a dividend distribution; (2) Since the 401(k) plan typically holds most of the stock of the C Corporation and dividend distributions are normally distributed pro-rata in the same ratio as the stock ownership is owned by the shareholders, the business owner normally does not have sufficient cash resources within the company to make the distributions pro-rata; and (3) Where will the cash come from? It is likely that the corporation spent all of the cash contributed to the company during the start-up period, and so may not be holding excess cash reserves.

Compliance costs associated with ROBS include the annual filing of Form 5500 (which the promoter will be glad to do for you for a fee of approximately $1,500) and you may need an annual valuation study of the business for ERISA reporting purposes. The cost of a valuation study will vary depending upon the business, but a range of $3,000 to $8,000 would not be an unreasonable amount to pay for a business valuation. If the valuation study must be performed each year, however, the cost to update the prior year's valuation study would be significantly less.

You can probably guess where we come down on the ROBS method of financing your business. But the difficulties go on—there are other issues to consider when the business is eventually sold. Let's assume that a ROBS transaction is done and the owner is very diligent and avoids any prohibited transactions, self-dealings, and does not discriminate against other participants in the 401(k) plan. The business has been successful and the owner now wishes to sell the business and use the sales proceeds to retire. Remember that the entrepreneur is not the owner of the business; the 401(k) is the owner (or at least the majority owner). Had the entrepreneur been the owner, he may have sold his business and reported the gain from the sale as a long-term capital gain, which currently is taxed at a lower rate than ordinary income. However, since the 401(k) is the owner, if the stock of the corporation is sold or if the assets of the business are sold, the 401(k) plan receives the sales proceeds. Those proceeds are put in the employees (entrepreneur's) 401(k) account, and when distributed to him, they will be taxed at ordinary income rates. The business owner has learned a costly lesson—he has turned capital gains income taxed at more favorable rates into ordinary income taxed at a higher tax rate.

Made in the USA
Middletown, DE
05 November 2015